IMMIGRATION

Tamara L. Roleff, *Book Editor*

Daniel Leone, *President*
Bonnie Szumski, *Publisher*
Scott Barbour, *Managing Editor*
Helen Cothran, *Senior Editor*

OPPOSING
VIEWPOINTS®
SERIES

GREENHAVEN
PRESS®

THOMSON
———✦———™
GALE

San Diego • Detroit • New York • San Francisco • Cleveland
New Haven, Conn. • Waterville, Maine • London • Munich

THOMSON
━━━━━━━✳━━━━━━━™
GALE

For more information, contact
Greenhaven Press
27500 Drake Rd.
Farmington Hills, MI 48331-3535
Or you can visit our Internet site at http://www.gale.com

LIBRARY OF CONGRESS CATALOGING-IN-PUBLICATION DATA
Immigration : opposing viewpoints in world history / Tamara L. Roleff, book editor.
   p. cm. — (Opposing viewpoints in world history series)
   Includes bibliographical references and index.
   ISBN 0-7377-1701-7 (lib. : alk. paper) — ISBN 0-7377-1702-5 (pbk. : alk. paper)
     1. United States—Emigration and immigration—Government policy—History.
   2. United States—Emigration and immigration—History. I. Roleff, Tamara L.,
   1959– . II. Series.
   JV6483.I5532 2004
   325.73—dc21
                                      2003053953

✸ Contents

United States in many areas, including the arts, science, industry, religion, politics, and vocabulary.

Chapter 3: The Golden Door Begins to Close

Scandinavia, and Germany—people whose cultures, ideals, and backgrounds are similar. Immigrants from other areas of Europe do not assimilate easily into this culture. Therefore, restricting the number of immigrants who are not Anglo-Saxon will give Americans time to help them assimilate.

Chapter 4: Looking Back at America's History of Immigration

grants settle together in ethnic enclaves and retain their
ethnic identity for several generations.

✳ Foreword

On December 2, 1859, several hundred soldiers gathered at the outskirts of Charles Town, Virginia, to carry out, and provide security for, the execution of a shabbily dressed old man with a beard that hung to his chest. The execution of John Brown quickly became and has remained one of those pivotal historical events that are immersed in controversy. Some of Brown's contemporaries claimed that he was a religious fanatic who deserved to be executed for murder. Others claimed Brown was a heroic and selfless martyr whose execution was a tragedy. Historians have continued to debate which picture of Brown is closest to the truth.

The wildly diverging opinions on Brown arise from fundamental disputes involving slavery and race. In 1859 the United States was becoming increasingly polarized over the issue of slavery. Brown believed in both the necessity of violence to end slavery and in the full political and social equality of the races. This made him part of the radical fringe even in the North. Brown's conviction and execution stemmed from his role in leading twenty-one white and black followers to attack and occupy a federal weapons arsenal in Harpers Ferry, Virginia. Brown had hoped to ignite a large slave uprising. However, the raid begun on October 16, 1859, failed to draw support from local slaves; after less than thirty-six hours, Brown's forces were overrun by federal and local troops. Brown was wounded and captured, and ten of his followers were killed.

Brown's raid—and its intent to arm slaves and foment insurrection—was shocking to the South and much of the North. An editorial in the *Patriot*, an Albany, Georgia, newspaper, stated that Brown was a "notorious old thief and murderer" who deserved to be hanged. Many southerners expressed fears that Brown's actions were part of a broader northern conspiracy against the South—fears that seemed to be confirmed by captured letters documenting Brown's ties with some prominent northern abolitionists, some of whom had provided him with financial support. Such alarms also found confirmation in the pronouncements of some speakers such as writer Henry David Thoreau, who asserted that

Brown had "a perfect right to interfere by force with the slave-holder, in order to rescue the slave." But not all in the North defended Brown's actions. Abraham Lincoln and William Seward, leading politicians of the nascent Republican Party, both denounced Brown's raid. Abolitionists, including William Lloyd Garrison, called Brown's adventure "misguided, wild, and apparently insane." They were afraid Brown had done serious damage to the abolitionist cause.

Today, though all agree that Brown's ideas on racial equality are no longer radical, historical opinion remains divided on just what Brown thought he could accomplish with his raid, or even whether he was fully sane. Historian Russell Banks argues that even today opinions of Brown tend to split along racial lines. African Americans tend to view him as a hero, Banks argues, while whites are more likely to judge him mad. "And it's for the same reason—because he was a white man who was willing to sacrifice his life to liberate Black Americans. The very thing that makes him seem mad to white Americans is what makes him seem heroic to Black Americans."

The controversy over John Brown's life and death remind readers that history is replete with debate and controversy. Not only have major historical developments frequently been marked by fierce debates as they happened, but historians examining the same events in retrospect have often come to opposite conclusions about their causes, effects, and significance. By featuring both contemporaneous and retrospective disputes over historical events in a pro/con format, the Opposing Viewpoints in World History series can help readers gain a deeper understanding of important historical issues, see how historical judgments unfold, and develop critical thinking skills. Each article is preceded by a concise summary of its main ideas and information about the author. An in-depth book introduction and prefaces to each chapter provide background and context. An annotated table of contents and index help readers quickly locate material of interest. Each book also features an extensive bibliography for further research, questions designed to spark discussion and promote close reading and critical thinking, and a chronology of events.

Introduction

The Myth vs. the Reality of Welcoming the Huddled Masses

Americans have had a love/hate relationship with immigration practically since the first colony was settled in the seventeenth century. During America's early years, immigrants—called colonists or settlers then—were needed and wanted to settle the vast regions of the new land. When King George III prevented immigrants from coming to the American colonies, the founding fathers listed his actions as one of their grievances in the Declaration of Independence: "He has endeavoured to prevent the Population of these States; by obstructing the Laws for Naturalization of Foreigners; refusing to pass others to encourage their Migrations hither, and raising the Conditions of new Appropriations of Lands."[1]

A century later, in 1883, Emma Lazarus wrote a poem, "The New Colossus," to raise funds to build the pedestal for the Statue of Liberty, a gift from France to celebrate America's first century of freedom and liberty. When the poem was engraved on the statue's pedestal, the line "Give me your tired, your poor, your huddled masses yearning to breathe free, the wretched refuse of your teeming shore"[2] soon transformed the Statue of Liberty from a symbol of freedom into an image of welcome to immigrants.

Yet at the same time that these sentiments were being expressed, other prominent Americans were unhappy that the world's "wretched refuse" was landing on America's shores. An editorial in the *Virginia Gazette* in 1751 complained that England was sending thieves and murderers to the colonies. Benjamin Franklin wrote in 1753, "Those who come hither are generally the most stupid of their own nation."[3] Thomas Hancock, the uncle of Declaration of Independence signer John Hancock, wrote in a letter in 1755, "For God's sake then let us Root the French blood out of America."[4] And in 1882 Congress passed the Chinese Exclusion Act, the first law that prevented a specific class and race of people from immigrating to the United States. These conflicting views of immigrants and immigration have continued into the twenty-first century.

The Beginning of Mass Immigration

There are few immigration records prior to 1820, which is when Congress passed a law ordering the collection of information about immigrants' countries of origin, genders, ages, and occupations. Most immigrants prior to 1820 were English, or Scotch Irish, and immigration was never very heavy; some estimates put the annual number at six thousand per year. The War of 1812 between England and the United States essentially halted immigration until the hostilities ended in 1815. In 1817 some federal documents show that 22,240 immigrants arrived in the United States; this was the highest-known annual figure up to that point.

Most Americans welcomed immigrants prior to the 1820s. People were needed to settle the country, and the majority of those who arrived shared the same ethnic background as the original settlers. In fact, throughout the 1800s some individual states and territories encouraged immigration; the states published glowing accounts of the wonders and bounty that could be found within their borders to attract immigrants. What grumbling there was about immigration concerned mainly the quality of the immigrants, who were mostly poor and unskilled laborers. There were few, if any, complaints about the quantity or heritage of the immigrants.

That was all soon to change, however, as what was once a trickle of new residents soon became a flood. Americans began to feel overwhelmed when an average of fifteen thousand immigrants arrived each year during the 1820s, more than sixty thousand per year during the 1830s, 170,000 annually in the 1840s, and 260,000 each year during the 1850s. Between 1815 and 1860, more than 5 million people immigrated to the United States—a number greater than the population of some European countries. These numbers count only those immigrants who arrived in steerage; first-class passengers did not have to go through customs and generally were not counted. Although 95 percent of these immigrants came from northern and western Europe, few were of the traditional English and Scotch Irish stock. Most were Irish, German, or Scandinavian. The exceedingly large number of Irish immigrants—1.5 to 2 million between 1840 and 1860—overwhelmed the Americans on the eastern seaboard. Despite these high numbers, more Americans can claim German ancestry than any other nationality. Germans made up 25 percent—or more—of all European immigrants between 1830 and 1880.

The Germans and Scandinavians who arrived on the East Coast of the United States tended to be a little better off than the Irish, so they were able to continue their migration westward to the north-central forests and the Midwestern prairie. The Germans and Scandinavians tended to move to rural areas where there may have been only a few other immigrant families. They were able to buy farms or establish businesses and soon settled into rural life. Although Germans experienced prejudice and discrimination because of their religion—Germans were Catholic and Jewish as well as Protestant—their dispersal into the rural country and their reputation for being hard workers helped enormously in their acceptance by Americans.

However, German immigrants were still accused of not assimilating into American society, in large part because many communities with a large German presence allowed schools to teach students in German instead of in English. By the turn of the twentieth century, however, anti-German sentiments forced public schools around the country to discontinue instruction in German. In Nebraska, for example, the provision allowing instruction in German was repealed in 1918 after it was denounced by the governor as "un-American." The next year, Nebraska forbade teachers in both public and private schools from teaching in any language other than English; nor could foreign languages be studied before the eighth grade. A Nebraska legislator expressed a sentiment popular at the time: "If these people are Americans, let them speak our language."[5] Although the U.S. Supreme Court overturned the Nebraska law in 1925, the harm to German private schools had already been done. The hundreds of thousands of students in German schools prior to World War I had dwindled to about seventeen thousand by 1936.

Whereas Americans initially welcomed German immigrants (until the anti-German hysteria of World War I), Irish immigrants had three strikes against them from the start: They were poor, they were illiterate, and they were Catholic. Although most immigrants to the United States had saved a little money for the journey, many Irish were forced to immigrate due to the potato blight of 1845 through 1847 and the subsequent starvation that killed millions. It was cheaper and easier for the English landlords to pay the fares for their poor Irish tenant farmers to immigrate to the United States than it was to support the relief programs for them. As a result, millions of destitute men, women, and children were forced to leave Ireland.

Thus, when the Irish arrived in the United States, they had no money to establish businesses, buy property, or travel westward to reach the areas of open farmland. Consequently, they tended to stay in urban areas—usually New York and Boston, where their ships had docked. Out of a desire to live with what was familiar, the immigrants clustered together in ethnic neighborhoods. However, poverty forced Irish families to live in crowded tenements in the slums, sharing small two- or three-room apartments with several other families. Because most Irish were illiterate and unskilled, the men were forced to take low-paying jobs such as digging ditches, sewers, and canals; laying pipes for gas and water; paving roads; building railroads; and mining coal. Women had few choices beyond domestic work. The work for both sexes was hard, and the hours were long. For the men, work was hazardous. Frequently, the working conditions were so bad that the men rioted, thus creating the reputation of the Irish as violent brawlers. Soon, employers began posting notices that "Irish need not apply" to their signs and advertisements for help.

The Rise of Nativism

Many Americans had been alarmed at the large number of Scandinavian and German immigrants that began arriving in the United States in the early 1800s, but it was not until the inunda-

tion of the Catholic Irish in the 1840s that these feelings fueled an
anti-immigrant political movement known as nativism. Nativists
favored long-term, or "native," U.S. residents over recent immigrants in employment and politics. Nativists believed—correctly,
in some cases—that the immigrants were taking jobs away from
them and that the immigrants' willingness to work for low pay
was driving down wages for everyone. Anti-immigration or nativist societies were formed to protect American workers from immigrants by preventing Catholics—and later other groups—from
entering the United States and by preventing those immigrants
already in the United States from participating in the political process by enacting long residency requirements for voting and election to office.

Catholics were especially feared by Protestant Americans, who
believed the pope would use his influence with Catholic immigrants to gain control of the federal and local governments. In
many cities on the East Coast, particularly New York and Boston,
which each had a large Irish immigrant population, the anti-
Catholic rhetoric became violent. Convents and churches were
burned, ransacked, and desecrated; and nuns and priests were often attacked and beaten by hostile Protestant nativists.

Because many of the newly arrived immigrants were poor and
could not find housing, afford to buy food, or arrange for transportation to other cities, the port cities where they arrived were
forced to provide for the poor. With immigrants arriving at greatly
increasing rates, the costs soon became staggering for the cities.
In response, many ports began to impose a head tax on immigrants—paid for by the shipowners—that would be used to support the poor and destitute immigrants. However, the U.S.
Supreme Court ruled in 1849 that these state laws were unconsti-
tutional; the Court declared that only Congress had the right to
regulate immigration. The Court's ruling led to more support for
the anti-immigrant movement. Various political parties—such as
the American Party (also known as the Know-Nothing Party because its members, when asked by outsiders about the workings
of the party, replied they knew nothing)—developed in the 1840s
and 1850s to prevent immigrants from voting and holding office.
The Know-Nothing platform called for a twenty-one-year resi-

dency before immigrants could become citizens and vote, and it sought to bar immigrants from all but the lowest political office.

The Civil War was largely responsible for the demise of the Know-Nothing Party. Americans became more concerned about the war between the states than about Catholics and poor immigrants who did not speak English. In addition, regiments of German and Irish immigrants were essential to the Union (and Confederate) cause. The Civil War was also responsible for a change in the laws governing U.S. citizenship. In 1790 Congress had passed a naturalization statute giving citizenship to any "free white person" who had lived in the United States for two years or more. The Fourteenth Amendment, ratified in 1868, provided that "all persons born or naturalized in the United States . . . are citizens of the United States and of the State wherein they reside."[6] The original intent of the amendment was to give the right to vote to the newly freed slaves, but it later created a conflict with the 1790 naturalization statute, which only granted citizenship to whites. The Fourteenth Amendment gave the right of citizenship to Asians who were born in the United States, but their parents could never, under current U.S. law, become citizens. Congress "fixed" this contradiction in 1870 by passing a law that allowed "white persons and persons of African descent" citizenship, denying all Asians the right to become U.S. citizens. Asians were now classified under a new category: aliens ineligible for citizenship.

Immigration from China

The change in U.S. naturalization laws came about due to the large numbers of Asians who were immigrating to the United States following the discovery of gold in California in 1848. Prior to 1840 there were about a dozen documented cases of Chinese immigrants entering the United States. By 1880 there were more than one hundred thousand Chinese immigrants in the United States, primarily on the West Coast. During the heyday of the gold rush, the Chinese immigrants were initially welcomed. They were hard workers who were willing to perform dangerous jobs in the mines and on the transcontinental railroad. In 1852 the governor of California asked Congress to allocate more land grants in the state in order to encourage more Chinese to immigrate since the Chinese were "one of the most worthy of our newly adopted citizens."[7]

But it was not long before Americans were no longer so welcoming to the Chinese. Chinese immigrants were almost entirely single men who left their families behind in China. The Chinese dressed differently, had unfamiliar customs, spoke an unrecognizable language, and sent most of their pay to their families still living in China. Their willingness to work at any job for low pay also made them a threat to American workers during economic hard times. Lee Chew, a Chinese immigrant in San Francisco during the 1880s, explains why Americans turned against the Chinese:

> It was the jealousy of laboring men of other nationalities—especially the Irish—that raised all the outcry against the Chinese. No one would hire an Irishman, German, Englishman or Italian when he could get a Chinese, because our countrymen are so much more honest, industrious, steady, sober and painstaking. Chinese were persecuted, not for their vices but for their virtues.[8]

California reversed course and tried to discourage Chinese workers from immigrating. When that did not work, the state began persecuting Chinese. In 1885 the state imposed a one-time entry tax of fifty-five dollars on every Chinese immigrant—a considerable sum back then—and in 1860 Chinese children were prohibited from attending California's public schools. Fees and taxes were imposed on laundries, traditional Chinese businesses in the United States. It also became a misdemeanor to carry goods in baskets suspended from a pole across the shoulders—a traditional Chinese method of transporting merchandise. Convicted criminals were required to cut their hair to a length of one inch, another attempt to humiliate the Chinese, who wore their hair in a long braid down their backs. Attacks against the Chinese were rarely investigated or punished by law enforcement officials. California also passed laws prohibiting businesses from employing Chinese workers and denying Chinese immigrants the right to vote.

Despite all this anti-Chinese sentiment on the West Coast, the United States signed the Burlingame Treaty in 1868, which opened up China to U.S. trade and guaranteed the Chinese the right to immigrate to the United States. However, the treaty did not allow Chinese immigrants to become naturalized American citizens, a right to which every other immigrant was entitled. Responding to complaints about Chinese immigration by American workers and labor unions—who believed that Chinese workers were taking jobs from Americans and forcing down their wages—Congress tried to pass laws beginning in the late 1870s banning immigration of Chinese laborers to the United States. The laws were successfully vetoed by three presidents because they violated the terms of the Burlingame Treaty, guaranteeing the right of the Chinese to immigrate to the United States. Finally, in 1880, the Burlingame Treaty was revised. The revised treaty gave the United States the right to "regulate, limit or suspend" immigration of Chinese laborers, but it did not allow it to "absolutely prohibit" Chinese immigration. This new treaty allowed Congress to override President Chester Arthur's veto of the Chinese Exclusion Act of 1882, which prohibited the immigration of all Chinese laborers for ten years. (Chinese immigrants who could prove they were merchants or had a professional trade were still allowed to enter the United States, but their numbers were few.) The Chinese Exclusion Act is a milestone in immigration history because it was the first time that immigrants were prohibited from coming to the United States because of their race. The bill was extended for another ten years in 1902 before it was made permanent in 1912. The act was finally repealed in 1943.

Following the passage of the Chinese Exclusion Act, other Asians began immigrating to the United States to fill the void left by the drop in Chinese immigrants. More than thirty thousand Japanese immigrants came to the United States in 1907, and the 1910 census reported 72,157 Japanese immigrants. Koreans and Filipinos also came to America to supply the need for cheap labor; their exact numbers are unknown as census records list them simply as "other Asians." Like the Chinese, however, the Japanese, Koreans, and Filipinos faced discrimination in the United States, to the point where the U.S. government declared all Asians ineligible for citizenship, revoked the citizenship of American women who married Asian men, and also prohibited noncitizens from buying land. President Theodore Roosevelt negotiated a treaty with Japan in 1907, called the Gentlemen's Agreement, in which Japan agreed not to issue any passports to the Japanese laborers to come to the United States. The agreement was soon obsolete, however, as Congress passed laws in the 1920s restricting immigration from Japan, Korea, and the Philippines.

A New Focus for an Old Argument

Whereas West Coast workers in the late 1800s were concerned about the influx of Asian laborers, East Coast residents were worried about the large number of immigrants from southern and eastern Europe who were arriving by the tens of thousands. These "new" European immigrants were very different from the "old" European immigrants of just a few decades earlier. The new immigrants were primarily from Italy, Poland, Greece, Russia, Turkey, and Austria-Hungary, whereas the old immigrants had come from England, Ireland, Germany, and Scandinavia. But the differences were more than geographic. The languages, culture, customs, and religion of the new immigrants were completely different from the Anglo-Saxon Protestants of western Europe, and the nativists began a new campaign to restrict European immigration.

The same arguments that had been used against the Irish in the 1840s were now turned on the new immigrants from southern and eastern Europe. Like the Irish before them (who had by the 1880s assimilated and were now considered to be hardworking Americans worthy of citizenship), the new immigrants were poor and unskilled and therefore willing to take whatever jobs they could find. Their willingness to work at undesirable, unskilled jobs led to fears that they threatened to lower American wages and the standard of living—the same argument that had been used against other immigrants for decades and even longer.

In addition, Americans in the big port cities—especially in New York—complained that they were overwhelmed by the large numbers of immigrants who were arriving—and staying—in their cities. During the 1880s, approximately 5.25 million immigrants entered the United States; nearly three-quarters of them landed in New York City, where the majority stayed. This inundation of immigrants—who were again different from what Americans were used to—gave rise to another period of nativist feeling beginning in the 1880s.

New nativist organizations were formed to protect the American worker from the immigrant threat. The American Protective Association (APA) was founded in 1887, and although it boasted more than five hundred thousand members by the 1890s, it was no more successful in changing immigration policy than the Know-Nothing Party of the pre–Civil War era. The APA was strongly anti-Catholic; the organization demanded that its members not vote for a Catholic candidate or hire Catholic workers. In addition, APA members worked unsuccessfully to pass laws that restricted admittance to Catholic immigrants. The American Federation of Labor was also strongly anti-immigrant. An advertisement printed by the labor union in the 1890s expressed the belief of many Americans when it asked, "We keep out pauper-made goods . . . why not keep out the pauper?"[9] In response, Congress passed a law in 1891 prohibiting the following classes of people from entering the United States: "all idiots, insane persons, paupers or persons likely to become a public charge, persons suffering from a contagious or loathsome disease, persons who have been convicted of a felony or other infamous crime or misdemeanor involving moral turpitude, and polygamists."[10]

By the 1890s the eugenics movement (whose adherents believed that the white race could be improved by careful breeding) was gaining popularity. Many of America's political and academic leaders became convinced that the Anglo-Saxon, Nordic, Teutonic, and Aryan "races" (the last three of which had been considered "undesirable" by nativists a few decades earlier) were superior to all other ethnic groups. Many Americans began working to restrict immigration to these "desirable" groups and prevent the "undesirable" groups from entering the country. Prescott F. Hall, one of the founders of the Immigration Restriction League (IRL, an influential anti-immigration organization founded in 1894), argued that Americans needed to decide if they wanted the United States "to be peopled by British, German and Scandinavian stock, historically free, energetic, progressive, or by Slav, Latin and Asiatic races [this latter referred to Jews rather than Chinese or Japanese] historically down-trodden, atavistic and stagnant."[11]

The IRL chose the literacy test as its principal method to prevent these "undesirable" immigrants from becoming U.S. residents.

The Literacy Test

The literacy test seemed to be the perfect solution to keep out the "undesirable" southern and eastern European immigrants. Like the Irish immigrants before them, the Slavic and Latin ethnic groups were largely poor and uneducated. The illiteracy rate was high among the southern and eastern Europeans; 35.4 percent of Polish immigrants, 54.2 percent of Italian immigrants, and 68.2 percent of Portuguese immigrants were illiterate, according to the Immigration Commission, while the illiteracy rate among Scandinavian, English, Irish, and German immigrants was .4, 1.1, 2.7, and 5.1 percent, respectively. Supporters of literacy tests knew that the tests would appear to be a "fair" method of testing immigrants but that the result would keep out many "undesirable" immigrants. They estimated that a quarter of all "undesirable" immigrants would be excluded if a literacy test were required.

In 1895 Henry Cabot Lodge, a U.S. senator from Massachusetts who vigorously supported the IRL and immigration restrictions, sponsored the first bill that would require all new immigrants to pass a literacy test given in their own language. Although the Senate did not pass the first bill, the House did, and both sides of Congress passed a literacy test bill in 1897, 1913, 1915, and 1917. However, Presidents Grover Cleveland, William Howard Taft, and Woodrow Wilson all vetoed the bills. Their reasons varied; Cleveland called the bill "illiberal, narrow, and un-American"[12] because it went against the American tradition of welcoming the oppressed. Taft noted in his veto in 1913 that literacy was the result of having opportunities, which were often denied to these immigrants in their home countries. By coming to the United States, he wrote, the immigrants were trying to better themselves, and therefore America should not deny them this opportunity. Wilson's veto in 1915 was along much the same lines; literacy tests, he wrote, "are not tests of quality or of character or of personal fitness, but tests of opportunity. Those who come seeking opportunity are not to be admitted unless they already had one of the chief opportunities they seek—the opportunity of education."[13]

Supporters of literacy tests were not deterred by the presidential vetoes. In 1917 Congress passed another bill, Wilson again vetoed it, but both houses of Congress finally found enough votes to override his veto. The Asia Barred Zone and Literacy Act (so called because the law also barred immigrants from almost all Asian countries) was America's strictest immigration law up to that point.

The literacy test actually had a limited effect on immigration, however. Due to the war in Europe, immigration numbers had already dropped to a third of what they had been before World War I. Also, the literacy test permitted immigrants to read a passage in any language they chose, including Hebrew and Yiddish. Furthermore, if a husband was literate, his wife was not required to be literate, although the reverse was not true. Of the more than eight hundred thousand immigrants who arrived in the United States from July 1920 to June 1921, only 1,450 were denied entrance due to the literacy test.

Supporters of immigration restrictions were finding that their piecemeal restrictions were having little effect on reducing the number of immigrants to the United States. Congress had added anarchists and others who advocated the overthrow of government to its list of excluded persons in 1918 when revolutions in Germany and Russia caused many Americans to fear political radicals. Yet despite the long list of excluded persons—paupers, prostitutes, criminals, Asians, the illiterate, radicals, and people who were immoral or who had contagious or loathsome diseases— fewer than thirteen thousand immigrants were refused entry in 1905, the first year that more than 1 million immigrants arrived in the United States. The number of immigrants who were returned to their home country was never very large—it consistently hovered around 1 to 2 percent of those who were allowed to enter. It was clear to the anti-immigrationists that the United States could not continue to accept a million immigrants a year and that all the restrictions currently in place were not working. A radical new measure to restrict immigration was needed.

The Quota Act

The response to the panic caused by the large immigration numbers was the introduction of the Dillingham Quota Act of 1920.

The act limited the total number of immigrants allowed to enter the United States in a year and then assigned a percentage of that total number to particular countries based on the number of people of that nationality already in the United States according to the census of 1910. The original quota bill—which passed in the Senate—called for a yearly limit of 600,000 immigrants, but a compromise between the Senate and House lowered the total number of immigrants to 350,000. The compromise also reduced each country's quota from 5 to 3 percent of the country's nationals in the United States in 1910. Countries with a high representation in the United States—such as Great Britain, Germany, and Scandinavian countries—would be allowed to send a larger number of immigrants to America than would countries with a lower representation—such as the "undesirable" countries.

However, the quota act did not perform quite as expected. The 1910 census included a large number of residents from Slavic and Latin countries, and so a large quota was allowed to enter as immigrants. When the Dillingham Quota Act was due to expire in 1924, Congress set about trying to "fix" this problem. By this time, the idea of restricting the numbers of immigrants to the United States was generally accepted, so the solution was just a matter of fiddling with the numbers. Congress therefore changed the census baseline to 1890, when the majority of immigrants had been from northern Europe and very few were from southern and eastern Europe. It also reduced the quota percentage from 3 to 2 percent of the immigrants' population in the United States. The changes in the quota law increased the number of immigrants allowed in from Great Britain, Germany, and Scandinavia, drastically reduced the number of immigrants from all other Eastern Hemisphere countries (no restrictions were placed on immigrants from Canada, Mexico, and other Western Hemisphere countries), and completely prohibited immigration from Japan. This was an intentional insult to Japan since, under the Gentlemen's Agreement of 1907, Japanese immigration had already been severely restricted to allow fewer than two hundred Japanese immigrants to enter the United States each year. The 1924 Quota Act remained essentially in place until 1965. The era of free immigration to the United States was officially over.

America's feelings of ambivalence about immigration are as much a part of American history as the arrival of the immigrants themselves. When times are good and jobs are plentiful, immigrants have been welcomed. During hard times, many Americans blame their problems on immigrants and try to enact laws to make it more difficult for immigrants to come to the United States. The authors in this historical anthology look at the issues involving immigration during its peak—from the 1820s to the implementation of the first quota laws in the 1920s. The authors' views on immigration reflect their beliefs about what makes a resident an American—whether it be ethnic heritage, long-term residency, the number of generations a family has lived in the United States, or participation in the political process. In the following chapters of *Immigration: Opposing Viewpoints in American History*, immigrants, politicians, authors, and contemporary commentators debate the many issues of immigration.

Notes

1. Declaration of Independence, July 4, 1776.
2. Emma Lazarus, *The Poems of Emma Lazarus*, vol. 1. Boston: Houghton, Mifflin, 1889, pp. 202–203.
3. Benjamin Franklin, *The Complete Works of Benjamin Franklin*, vol. 2. New York: Putnam, 1887–1888, p. 291.
4. Quoted in William Threipland Baxter, *House of Hancock*. Cambridge, MA: Harvard University Press, 1945, p. 132.
5. Quoted in Roger Daniels, *Coming to America: A History of Immigration and Ethnicity in American Life*, 2nd ed. New York: Perennial, 2002, p. 160.
6. U.S. Constitution, amend. 14.
7. Quoted in Dennis Wepman, *Immigration: From the Founding of Virginia to the Closing of Ellis Island*. New York: Facts On File, 2002, p. 138.
8. Quoted in Wepman, *Immigration*, p. 192.
9. Quoted in Wepman, *Immigration*, p. 178.
10. Quoted in Daniels, *Coming to America*, p. 274.
11. Quoted in Daniels, *Coming to America*, p. 276.
12. Quoted in Wepman, *Immigration*, p. 219.
13. Quoted in Wepman, *Immigration*, p. 221.

CHAPTER 1

The First Wave: The 1820s to 1860s

✵ Chapter Preface

In the early nineteenth century, life in rural Ireland became even more difficult than it already was. Most Irish farmers did not own their own land but rented small crop fields from the Irish gentry. A depression lowered the prices farmers received for their crops and made it nearly impossible for many to pay their rents, taxes, and church tithes, resulting in the evictions of thousands from their little plots of land. When beef prices rose, making it more profitable to raise cattle than crops, many of the landed gentry evicted their poor tenant farmers in order to convert crop fields into pastures. Potatoes became the salvation of millions of Irish people; they were easily grown, nutritious, and abundant enough to stave off starvation for three-quarters of Ireland's population.

However, beginning in 1845, a potato blight devastated Ireland's potato crop. Unable to pay their landlords, hundreds of thousands of peasants were evicted from their homes and millions of people starved to death. The Protestant British government did little or nothing to ease the famine, for many British officials believed that the Irish—most of whom were Catholic—were immoral and undeserving of aid. Although Ireland had other crops that could have fed a population twice its size, the British government exported most of its food to other parts of the world under military guard. Furthermore, the British hoped that English and Scottish farmers—who were Protestant and loyal to the Crown—would move to Ireland to replace the dying Irish farmers. As a result of the potato famine and British policies, approximately 30 percent of Ireland's population emigrated in a ten-year period, mostly to the United States.

Soon after the Irish migration to the United States came the Germans. Modernization, population growth, and distress over government policies following a failed revolution in 1848–1849 fueled the massive migration. More than 4.5 million German immigrants arrived in the United States between 1840 and 1890; more Americans claim German ancestors than any other nationality. A large number of German immigrants were also Catholic, and "even worse" (according to the established Americans), they spoke German instead of English.

Once in the United States, both the Irish and the Germans tended to settle near their compatriots, forming areas of "Little Ireland" or "Little Germany." The Irish often formed their own schools in order to pass on their religious beliefs. The Germans also formed their own schools where their children were taught in German as opposed to English. Because these two immigrant groups immigrated in such large numbers, settled in ethnic clusters, formed their own schools, were Catholic instead of Protestant, and, in the case of Germans, spoke a different language, their presence provoked hostile and strong nativist reactions from Americans. The Irish and Germans were distrusted and feared, and it was widely believed that they were not able to assimilate into American culture.

For these reasons, many Americans began to speak out against unlimited immigration and agitate for restrictions on the number of immigrants, especially on those—such as the Irish and Germans—who were different from the white, Anglo-Saxon Protestants who made up the majority of the country's population at the beginning of the nineteenth century. Nevertheless, poor Europeans, especially the Irish and the Germans who had few alternatives and little hope in their homelands, saw America as the land of opportunity and came to the United States to make a better life for themselves. The authors in this chapter debate the issues raised by this "first wave" of immigrants.

Viewpoint 1

"The danger of foreign influence, threatening the gradual destruction of our national institutions . . . has awakened deep alarm in the mind of every intelligent patriot, from the days of Washington to the present time."

Immigrants Endanger America

Native American Party

Hundreds of thousands of immigrants—many of whom were Catholic—poured into the United States during the first half of the nineteenth century. Many Americans felt overwhelmed and threatened by the large number of foreigners landing on their shores. In response, anti-immigrationists formed political organizations founded on the principle of nativism, a movement devoted to the idea that immigrants threatened the economic and political security of "native" Americans—white, Anglo-Saxon Protestants. One such organization, the Native American Party, founded in 1844, helped dozens of candidates get elected to office in New York, Pennsylvania, and Massachusetts that year. The candidates and their followers were committed to keeping America free of immigrant influences by electing only "native" Americans and requiring twenty-five years' residency for citizenship.

The Native American Party held its first national convention

Native American Party, National Platform, 1845.

in Philadelphia in 1845 and adopted a platform that outlined the threats it believed immigrants posed to the country. The following viewpoint is excerpted from that platform. The members were convinced that the United States was in imminent peril from immigrants, many of whom they believed were insane, feeble, paupers, or criminals. Anti-immigrationists were also concerned that the new immigrants would band together with no desire to assimilate into American culture. Americans and American institutions would thus be endangered by adopted citizens who would place their foreign interests above American interests. Therefore, the anti-immigrationists believed that strict controls should be placed on immigration.

We, the delegates elect to the first National Convention of the Native American body of the United States of America, assembled at Philadelphia, on the 4th of July, A.D. 1845, for the purpose of devising a plan of concerted political action in defence of American institutions against the encroachments of foreign influence, open or concealed, hereby solemnly, and before Almighty God, make known to our fellow citizens, our country, and the world, the following incontrovertible facts, and the course of conduct consequent thereon, to which, in duty to the cause of human rights and the claims of our beloved country, we mutually pledge our lives, our fortunes, and our sacred honour.

The danger of foreign influence, threatening the gradual destruction of our national institutions, failed not to arrest the attention of the Father of his Country, in the very dawn of American Liberty. Not only its direct agency in rendering the American system liable to the poisonous influence of European policy—a policy at war with the fundamental principles of the American Constitution—but also its still more fatal operation in aggravating the virulence of partisan warfare—has awakened deep alarm in the mind of every intelligent patriot, from the days of Washington to the present time.

The influx of a foreign population, permitted after little more than a nominal residence, to participate in the legislation of the country and the sacred right of suffrage, produced comparatively little evil during the earlier years of the Republic; for that influx was then limited by the considerable expenses of a transatlantic voyage, by the existence of many wholesome restraints upon the acquisition of political prerogatives, by the constant exhaustion of the European population in long and bloody continental wars, and by the slender inducements offered for emigration to a young and sparsely peopled country, contending for existence with a boundless wilderness, inhabited by savage men. Evils which are only prospective rarely attract the notice of the masses, and until peculiar changes in the political condition of Europe, the increased facilities for transportation, and the madness of partisan legislation in removing all effective guards against the open prostitution of the right of citizenship had converted the slender current of naturalization into a torrent threatening to overwhelm the influence of the natives of the land, the far-seeing vision of the statesman, only, being fixed upon the distant, but steadily approaching, cloud.

But, since the barriers against the improper extension of the right of suffrage were bodily broken down, for a partisan purpose, by the Congress of 1825, the rapidly increasing numbers and unblushing insolence of the foreign population of the worst classes have caused the general agitation of the question, "How shall the institutions of the country be preserved from the blight of foreign influence, insanely legalized through the conflicts of domestic parties?" Associations under different names have been formed by our fellow citizens, in many States of this confederation, from Louisiana to Maine, all designed to check this imminent danger before it becomes irremediable, and, at length, a National Convention of the great American people, born upon the soil of Washington, has assembled to digest and announce a plan of operation, by which the grievances of an abused hospitality, and the consequent degradation of political morals, may be redressed, and the tottering columns of the temple of Republican Liberty secured upon the sure foundation of an enlightened nationality.

In calling for support upon every American who loves his country pre-eminently, and every adopted citizen of moral and intellectual worth who would secure, to his compatriots yet to come amongst us, the blessings of political protection, the safety of person and property, it is right that we should make known the grievances which we propose to redress, and the manner in which we shall endeavour to effect our object.

Imminent Peril

It is an incontrovertible truth that the civil institutions of the United States of America have been seriously affected, and that they now stand in imminent peril from the rapid and enormous increase of the body of residents of foreign birth, imbued with foreign feelings, and of an ignorant and immoral character, who receive, under the present lax and unreasonable laws of naturalization, the elective franchise and the right of eligibility to political office.

The whole body of foreign citizens, invited to our shores under a constitutional provision adapted to other times and other political conditions of the world, and of our country especially, has been endowed by American hospitality with gratuitous privileges unnecessary to the enjoyment of those inalienable rights of man— life, liberty, and the pursuit of happiness—privileges wisely reserved to the Natives of the soil by the governments of all other civilized nations. But, familiarized by habit with the exercise of these indulgences, and emboldened by increasing numbers, a vast majority of those who constitute this foreign body, now claim as an original right that which has been so incautiously granted as a favour—thus attempting to render inevitable the prospective action of laws adopted upon a principle of mere expediency, made variable at the will of Congress by the express terms of the Constitution, and heretofore repeatedly revised to meet the exigencies of the times.

In former years, this body was recruited chiefly from the victims of political oppression, or the active and intelligent mercantile adventurers of other lands; and it then constituted a slender representation of the best classes of the foreign population well fitted to add strength to the state, and capable of being readily educated in the peculiarly American science of political self-government. Moreover, while welcoming the stranger of every condition, laws then wisely demanded of every foreign aspirant for political rights a certificate of practical good citizenship. Such a class of aliens were followed by no foreign demagogues—they were courted by no domestic demagogues; they were purchased by no parties—they were debauched by no emissaries of kings. A wall of fire separated them from such a baneful influence, erected by their intelligence, their knowledge, their virtue and love of freedom. But for the last twenty years the road to civil preferment and participation in the legislative and executive government of the land has been laid broadly open, alike to the ignorant, the vicious and the criminal; and a large proportion of the foreign body of citizens and voters now constitutes a representation of the worst and most degraded of the European population—victims of social oppression or personal vices, utterly divested, by ignorance or crime, of the moral and intellectual requisites for political self-government.

U.S. Policy Allows in the Criminal and Idle

Thus tempted by the suicidal policy of these United States, and favoured by the facilities resulting from the modern improvements of navigation, numerous societies and corporate bodies in foreign countries have found it economical to transport to our shores, at public and private expense, the feeble, the imbecile, the idle, and intractable, thus relieving themselves of the burdens resulting from the vices of the European social systems by availing themselves of the generous errors of our own.

The almshouses of Europe are emptied upon our coast, and this by our own invitation—not casually, or to a trivial extent, but systematically, and upon a constantly increasing scale. The Bedlams [insane asylums] of the old world have contributed their share to the torrent of immigration, and the lives of our citizens have been attempted in the streets of our capital cities by mad-men, just liberated from European hospitals upon the express condition that they should be transported to America. By the orders of European governments, the punishment of crimes has been commuted for banishment to the land of the free; and criminals in iron have crossed the ocean to be cast loose upon society on their arrival upon our shores. The United States are rapidly becoming the lazar house and penal colony of Europe; nor can we reasonably censure such proceedings. They are legitimate consequences of our own unlimited benevolence; and it is of such material that we profess to manufacture free and enlightened citizens, by a process occupying five short years at most, but practically oftentimes embraced in a much shorter period of time.

The mass of foreign voters, formerly lost among the Natives of the soil, has increased from the ratio of 1 in 40 to that of 1 in 7! A like advance in fifteen years will leave the Native citizens a minority in their own land! Thirty years ago these strangers came by units and tens—now they swarm by thousands. Formerly, most of them sought only for an honest livelihood and a provision for their families, and rarely meddled with the institutions, of which it was impossible they could comprehend the nature; now each newcomer seeks political preferment, and struggles to fasten on the public purse with an avidity, in strict proportion to his ignorance and unworthiness of public trust—having been sent for the purpose of obtaining political ascendancy in the government of the nation; having been sent to exalt their allies to power; having been sent to work a revolution from republican freedom to the divine rights of monarchs.

From these unhappy circumstances has arisen an *Imperium in Imperio*—a body uninformed and vicious—foreign in feeling, prejudice, and manner, yet armed with a vast and often a controlling influence over the policy of a nation, whose benevolence it abuses, and whose kindness it habitually insults; a body as dangerous to the rights of the intelligent foreigner as to the prospect of its own immediate progeny, as it is threatening to the liberties of the country, and the hopes of rational freedom throughout the world; a body ever ready to complicate our foreign relations by embroiling us with the hereditary hates and feuds of other lands, and to disturb our domestic peace by its crude ideas, mistaking license for liberty, and the overthrow of individual rights for republican political equality; a body ever the ready tool of foreign and domestic demagogues, and steadily endeavouring by misrule to establish popular tyranny under a cloak of false democracy. Americans, false to their country, and led on to moral crime by the desire of dishonest gain, have scattered their agents over Europe, inducing the malcontent and the unthrifty to exchange a life of compulsory labour in foreign lands for relative comfort, to be maintained by the tax-paying industry of our overburdened and deeply indebted

No Irish Need Apply

The Irish were one of the largest groups of immigrants to the United States. Some sources say that more than 2 million Irish immigrants came to the country between 1820 (when official immigration records were first kept) and 1860, with nearly 1 million arriving during the 1850s. Because of their large numbers, their poverty, and their Catholic religion, the Irish faced much hostility in the large cities where they tended to congregate after arriving in America. The following song illustrates the insults and anti-Irish sentiments the immigrants were forced to endure during this time.

I'm a decent boy just landed from the town of Ballyfad;
I want a situation and I want it very bad.
I've seen employment advertised, "It's just the thing," says I,
But the dirty spalpeen ended with "No Irish Need Apply."
"Whoo," says I, "that is an insult, but to get the place I'll try,"
So I went there to see the blackguard with his "No Irish Need Apply."

> *Chorus:*
> Some do think it is a misfortune to be christened Pat or Dan,
> But to me it is an honor to be born an Irishman.

I started out to find the house, I got there mighty soon;
I found the old chap seated—he was reading the *Tribune.*
I told him what I came for, when he in a rage did fly;
"No!" he says, "You are a Paddy, and no Irish need apply."
Then I gets my dander rising, and I'd like to black his eye
For to tell an Irish gentleman "No Irish Need Apply."

I couldn't stand it longer so a-hold of him I took,
And I gave him such a welting as he'd get at Donnybrook.
He hollered "Milia Murther," and to get away did try,
And swore he'd never write again "No Irish Need Apply."
Well, he made a big apology; I told him then goodbye,
Saying, "When next you want a beating, write 'No Irish Need Apply.'"

"No Irish Need Apply," in Encyclopaedia Britannica, *The Annals of America: Vol. 7: 1841–1849 Manifest Destiny.* Chicago: Encyclopaedia Britannica, 1976, p. 421.

community. Not content with the usual and less objectionable licenses of trade, these fraudulent dealers habitually deceive a worthier class of victims, by false promises of employment, and assist in thronging the already crowded avenues of simple labour with a host of competitors, whose first acquaintance with American faith springs from a gross imposture, and whose first feeling on discovering the cheat is reasonable mistrust, if not implacable revenge. The importation of the physical necessities of life is burdened with imposts which many deem extravagant; but the importation of vice and idleness—of seditious citizens and factious rulers—is not only unrestricted by anything beyond a nominal tax, but is actually encouraged by a system which transforms the great patrimony of the nation, purchased by the blood of our fathers, into a source of bounty for the promotion of immigration.

Fatal Evil

Whenever an attempt is made to restrain this fatal evil, the native and adopted demagogues protest against an effort which threatens to deprive them of their most important tools; and such is the existing organization of our established political parties, that should either of them essay the reform of an abuse which both acknowledge to be fraught with ruin, that party sinks upon the instant into a minority, divested of control, and incapable of result.

From such causes has been derived a body, armed with political power, in a country of whose system it is ignorant, and for whose institutions it feels little interest, except for the purpose of personal advancement. . . .

The body of adopted citizens, with foreign interests and prejudices, is annually advancing with rapid strides, in geometrical progression. Already it has acquired a control over our elections which cannot be entirely corrected, even by the wisest legislation, until the present generation shall be numbered with the past. Already it has notoriously swayed the course of national legislation, and invaded the purity of local justice. In a few years its unchecked progress would cause it to outnumber the native defenders of our rights, and would then inevitably dispossess our offspring, and its own, of the inheritance for which our fathers bled, or plunge this land of happiness and peace into the horrors of civil war.

The correction of these evils can never be effected by any combination governed by the tactics of other existing parties. If either of the old parties, as such, were to attempt an extension of the term of naturalization, it would be impossible for it to carry out the measure, because they would immediately be abandoned by the foreign voters. This great measure can be carried out only by an organization like our own, made up of those who have given up their former political preferences.

For these reasons, we recommend the immediate organization of the truly patriotic native citizens throughout the United States, for the purpose of resisting the progress of foreign influence in the conduct of American affairs, and the correction of such political abuses as have resulted from unguarded or partisan legislation on the subject of naturalization, so far as these abuses admit of remedy without encroachment upon the vested rights of foreigners who have been already legally adopted into the bosom of the nation.

Viewpoint 2

"The emigration of foreigners to this country is not only defensible on grounds of abstract justice . . . but . . . it has been in various ways highly beneficial to this country."

Immigrants Do Not Endanger America

Thomas L. Nichols

Although many Americans supported the nativist movement of anti-immigration, many others defended immigration. One such defender was Thomas L. Nichols, a doctor, social historian, and journalist, who gave a speech in New York in 1845 in which he defended a person's right to emigrate from one country to another. Nichols contends in the following viewpoint that those who have decided to immigrate are usually the best candidates for making a new life in a strange land—people who are strong-minded, brave, enterprising, and intelligent—and their efforts at making a new life in America have resulted in great contributions to the United States in terms of both wealth and labor. Furthermore, Nichols argues that Americans have little reason to fear "foreign influence" at the ballot box since most immigrants feel exceedingly loyal and patriotic toward their new country. Many immigrants were oppressed in their homeland and are therefore able to appreciate the glorious freedom in their new land.

Thomas L. Nichols, speech, New York, 1845.

The questions connected with emigration from Europe to America are interesting to both the old world and the new— are of importance to the present and future generations. They have more consequence than a charter or a state election; they involve the destinies of millions; they are connected with the progress of civilization, the rights of man, and providence of God!

I have examined this subject the more carefully, and speak upon it the more earnestly, because I have been to some extent, in former years, a partaker of the prejudices I have since learned to pity. A native of New England and a descendant of the puritans, I early imbibed, and to some extent promulgated, opinions of which reflection and experience have made me ashamed. . . .

But while I would speak of the motives of men with charity, I claim the right to combat their opinions with earnestness. Believing that the principles and practices of Native Americanism are wrong in themselves, and are doing wrong to those who are the objects of their persecution, justice and humanity require that their fallacy should be exposed, and their iniquity condemned. It may be unfortunate that the cause of the oppressed and persecuted, in opinion if not in action, has not fallen into other hands; yet, let me trust that the truth, even in mine, will prove mighty, prevailing from its own inherent power!

The Right to Emigrate

The right of man to emigrate from one country to another, is one which belongs to him by his own constitution and by every principle of justice. It is one which no law can alter, and no authority destroy. "Life, liberty, and the pursuit of happiness" are set down, in our Declaration of Independence, as among the self-evident, unalienable rights of man. If I have a right to live, I have also a right to what will support existence—food, clothing, and shelter. If then the country in which I reside, from a superabundant population, or any other cause, does not afford me these, my right to go from it to some other is self-evident and unquestionable. The *right to live*, then, supposes the right of emigration. . . .

I proceed, therefore, to show that the emigration of foreigners to this country is not only defensible on grounds of abstract justice—what we have no possible right to prevent, but that it has been in various ways highly beneficial to this country.

Emigration first peopled this hemisphere with civilized men. The first settlers of this continent had the same right to come here that belongs to the emigrant of yesterday—no better and no other. They came to improve their condition, to escape from oppression, to enjoy freedom—for the same, or similar, reasons as now prevail. And so far as they violated no private rights, so long as they obtained their lands by fair purchase, or took possession of those which were unclaimed and uncultivated, the highly respectable natives whom the first settlers found here had no right to make any objections. The peopling of this continent with civilized men, the cultivation of the earth, the various processes of productive labor, for the happiness of man, all tend to "the greatest good of the greatest number," and carry out the evident design of Nature or Providence in the formation of the earth and its inhabitants.

Emigration from various countries in Europe to America, producing a mixture of races, has had, and is still having, the most important influence upon the destinies of the human race. It is a principle, laid down by every physiologist, and proved by abundant observation, that man, like other animals, is improved and brought to its highest perfection by an intermingling of the blood and qualities of various races. That nations and families deteriorate from an opposite course has been observed in all ages. The great physiological reason why Americans are superior to other nations in freedom, intelligence, and enterprize, is because that they are the offspring of the greatest intermingling of races. The mingled blood of England has given her predominance over several nations of Europe in these very qualities, and a newer infusion, with favorable circumstances of climate, position, and institutions, has rendered Americans still superior. The Yankees of New England would never have shown those qualities for which they have been distinguished in war and peace throughout the world had there not been mingled with the puritan English, the calculating Scotch, the warm hearted Irish, the gay and chivalric French, the steady persevering Dutch, and the transcendental Germans, for all these nations contributed to make up the New England character, before the Revolution, and ever since to influence that of the whole American people.

America's Destiny Is to Be Peopled with Immigrants

It is not too much to assert that in the order of Providence this vast and fertile continent was reserved for this great destiny; to be the scene of this mingling of the finest European races, and consequently of the highest condition of human intelligence, freedom, and happiness; for I look upon this mixture of the blood and qualities of various nations, and its continual infusion, as absolutely requisite to the perfection of humanity. . . . Continual emigration, and a constant mixing of the blood of different races, is highly conducive to physical and mental superiority.

This country has been continually benefited by the immense amount of capital brought hither by emigrants. There are very few who arrive upon our shores without some little store of wealth, the hoard of years of industry. Small as these means may be in each case, they amount to millions in the aggregate, and every dollar is so much added to the wealth of the country, to be reckoned at compound interest from the time of its arrival, nor are these sums like our European loans, which we must pay back, both principal and interest. Within a few years, especially, and more or less at all periods, men of great wealth have been among the emigrants driven from Europe, by religious oppression or political revolutions. Vast sums have also fallen to emigrants and their descendants by inheritance, for every few days we read in the papers of some poor foreigner, or descendant of foreigners, as are we all, becoming the heir of a princely fortune, which in most cases, is added to the wealth of his adopted country. Besides this, capital naturally follows labor, and it flows upon this country in a constant current, by the laws of trade.

But it is not money alone that adds to the wealth of a country, but every day's productive labor is to be added to its accumulating capital. Every house built, every canal dug, every railroad graded, has added so much to the actual wealth of society; and who have built more houses, dug more canals, or graded more railroads, than the hardy Irishmen? I hardly know how our great national works could have been carried on without them—then; while every pair of sturdy arms has added to our national wealth, every hungry mouth has been a home market for our agriculture, and every broad shoulder has been clothed with our manufactures.

Europe's Most Valuable Members

From the very nature of the case, America gets from Europe the most valuable of her population. Generally, those who come here are the very ones whom a sensible man would select. Those who are attached to monarchical and aristocratic institutions stay at home where they can enjoy them. Those who lack energy and enterprize can never make up their minds to leave their native land. It is the strong minded, the brave hearted, the free and self-respecting, the enterprizing and the intelligent, who break away from all the ties of country and of home, and brave the dangers of the ocean, in search of liberty and independence, for themselves and for their children, on a distant continent; and it is from this, among other causes, that the great mass of the people of this country are distinguished for the very qualities we should look for in emigrants. The same spirit which sent our fathers across the ocean impels us over the Alleghanies, to the valley of the Mississippi, and thence over the Rocky mountains into Oregon.

For what are we not indebted to foreign emigration, since we are all Europeans or their descendants? We cannot travel on one of our steamboats without remembering that Robert Fulton was the son of an Irishman. We cannot walk by St. Paul's churchyard without seeing the monuments which admiration and gratitude have erected to Emmet, and Montgomery. Who of the thousands who every summer pass up and down our great thoroughfare, the North River, fails to catch at least a passing glimpse of the column erected to the memory of Kosciusko? I cannot forget that only last night a portion of our citizens celebrated with joyous festivities the birthday of the son of Irish emigrants, I mean the Hero of New Orleans!

Who speaks contemptuously of Alexander Hamilton as a foreigner, because he was born in one of the West India Islands? Who at this day will question the worth or patriotism of Albert Gallatin [appointed U.S. secretary of the treasury by President Thomas Jefferson, Gallatin helped arrange to make the Louisiana Purchase] because he first opened his eyes among the Alps of Switzerland— though, in fact, this was brought up and urged against him, when he was appointed special minister to Russia by James Madison. What New Yorker applies the epithet of "degraded foreigner" to the German immigrant, John Jacob Astor, a man who has spread his canvas on every sea, drawn to his adopted land the wealth of every clime, and given us, it may be, our best claim to vast territories!

Who would have banished the Frenchman, Stephen Girard, who, after accumulating vast wealth from foreign commerce, endowed with it magnificent institutions for education in his adopted land? So might I go on for hours, citing individual examples of benefits derived by this country from foreign immigration. . . .

I have enumerated some of the advantages which such emigration has given to America. Let us now very carefully inquire, whether there is danger of any injury arising from these causes, at all proportionable to the palpable good.

"Our country is in danger," is the cry of Nativism. During my brief existence I have seen this country on the very verge of ruin a considerable number of times. It is always in the most imminent peril every four years; but, hitherto, the efforts of one party or the other have proved sufficient to rescue it, just in the latest gasp of its expiring agonies, and we have breathed more freely, when we have been assured that "the country's safe." Let us look steadily in the face of this new danger.

Are foreigners coming here to overturn our government? Those who came before the Revolution appear to have been generally favorable to Republican institutions. Those who have come here since have left friends, home, country, all that man naturally holds dearest, that they might live under a free government—they and their children. Is there common sense in the supposition that men would voluntarily set about destroying the very liberties they came so far to enjoy?

"But they lack intelligence," it is said. Are the immigrants of to-day less intelligent than those of fifty or a hundred years ago? Has Europe and the human race stood still all this time? . . . The facts of men preferring this country to any other, of their desire to live under its institutions, of their migration hither, indicate to my mind anything but a lack of proper intelligence and enterprize. It has been charged against foreigners, by a portion of the whig press, that they generally vote with the democratic party. Allowing this to be so, I think that those who reflect upon the policy of the two parties, from the time of John Adams down to that of Mayor Harper, will scarcely bring this up as the proof of a lack of intelligence!

Immigrant Patriots

The truth is, a foreigner who emigrates to this country comes here saying, "Where Liberty dwells, there is my country." He sees our free institutions in the strong light of contrast. The sun seems brighter, because he has come out of darkness. What we know by hearsay only of the superiority of our institutions, he knows by actual observation and experience. Hence it is that America has had no truer patriots—freedom no more enthusiastic admirers—the cause of Liberty no more heroic defenders, than have been found among our adopted citizens. . . .

But if naturalized citizens of foreign birth had the disposition, they have not the power, to endanger our liberties, on account of their comparatively small and decreasing numbers. There appears to be a most extraordinary misapprehension upon this subject. To read one of our "Native" papers one might suppose that our country was becoming overrun by foreigners, and that there was real danger of their having a majority of votes. . . .

There is a point beyond which immigration cannot be carried. It must be limited by the capacity of the vessels employed in bringing passengers, while our entire population goes on increasing in geometrical progression, so that in one century from now, we shall have a population of one hundred and sixty millions, but a few hundred thousands of whom at the utmost can be citizens of foreign birth. Thus it may be seen that foreign immigration is of very little account, beyond a certain period, in the population of a country, and at all times is an insignificant item. . . .

In the infancy of this country the firstborn native found himself among a whole colony of foreigners. Now, the foreigner finds himself surrounded by as great a disproportion of natives, and the native babe and newly landed foreigner have about the same amount, of either power or disposition, to endanger the country in which they have arrived; one, because he chose to come—the other because he could not help it.

I said the power or the disposition, for I have yet to learn that foreigners, whether German or Irish, English or French, are at all disposed to do an injury to the asylum which wisdom has prepared and valor won for the oppressed of all nations and religions. I appeal to the observation of every man in this community, whether the Germans and the Irish here, and throughout the country, are not as orderly, as industrious, as quiet, and in the habit of performing as well the common duties of citizens as the great mass of natives among us.

The worst thing that can be brought against any portion of our foreign population is that in many cases they are poor, and when they sink under labor and privation, they have no resources but the almshouse. Alas! shall the rich, for whom they have labored, the owners of the houses they have helped to build, refuse to treat them as kindly as they would their horses when incapable of further toil? Can they grudge them shelter from the storm, and a place where they may die in peace?

Viewpoint 3

"America for the Americans—to shape and to govern; to make great, and to keep great, strong and free, from home foes and foreign demagogues and hierarchs."

America Belongs to Americans

New York Mirror

The following viewpoint was originally published as an editorial in an early newspaper, the *New York Mirror*, and later included in a book published in 1855 by an anti-immigrant, anti-Catholic American party known as the Know-Nothing Party. (The party's name came about because its members, when asked about the party, would reply that they knew nothing about it.) The editors argue that America should belong to Americans and that foreigners should not be permitted to hold public office, become citizens, or vote. In addition, the editors write that immigrants should not be allowed to form foreign regiments or battalions or benevolent, social, or other chartered organizations. Furthermore, all laws should be printed in English and children should be taught in English.

New York Mirror, "The Wide Awake Gift: A Know-Nothing Token for 1855," *New York Mirror*, 1855.

"America for Americans!"

Well, why not? Is there another country under the sun, that does not belong to its own native-born people? Is there another country where the alien by birth, and often by openly boasted sympathy, is permitted to fill the most responsible offices, and preside over the most sacred trusts of the land? Is there another country that would place its secret archives and its diplomacy with foreign states, in other than native hands—with tried and trusty native hearts to back them? Is there another country that would even permit the foreigner to become a citizen, shielded by its laws and its flag, on terms such as we exact, leaving the political franchise out of sight? More than all else, is there a country, other than ours, that would acknowledge as a citizen, a patriot, a republican, or a safe man, one who stood bound by a religious oath or obligation, in political conflict with, and which he deemed temporarily higher than, the Constitution and Civil Government of that country—to which he also professes to swear fealty?

America for the Americans, we say. And why not? Didn't they plant it, and battle for it through bloody revolution—and haven't they developed it, as only Americans could, into a nation of a century and yet mightier than the oldest empire on earth? Why shouldn't they shape and rule the destinies of their own land—the land of their birth, their love, their altars, and their graves; the land red and rich with the blood and ashes, and hallowed by the memories of their fathers? Why not rule their own, particularly when the alien betrays the trust that should never have been given him, and the liberties of the land are thereby imperilled?

The Majority Should Rule

Lacks the American numbers, that he may not rule by the right of majority, to which is constitutionally given the political sovereignty of this land? Did he not, at the last numbering of the people, count seventeen and a half millions, native to the soil, against less than two and a half millions of actually foreign-born, and those born of foreigners coming among us for the last three-quarters of a century? Has he not tried the mixed rule, with a tolerance unexampled, until it has plagued him worse than the lice and locust plagued the Egyptian? Has he not shared the trust of office and council, until foreign-born pauperism, vice and crime, stain the whole land—until a sheltered alien fraction have become rampant in their ingratitude and insolence? Has he not suffered burdens of tax, and reproach, and shame, by his ill-bestowed division of political power?

America for the Americans! That is the watchword that should ring through the length and breadth of the land, from the lips of the whole people. America for the Americans—to shape and to govern; to make great, and to keep great, strong and free, from home foes and foreign demagogues and hierarchs. In the hour of Revolutionary peril, [George] Washington said, "Put none but Americans on guard to-night." At a later time, [Thomas] Jefferson wished "an ocean of fire rolled between the Old World and the New." To their children, the American people, the fathers and builders of the Republic, bequeathed it. "Eternal vigilance is the price of liberty!"—let the American be vigilant that the alien seize not his birth-right.

We Must End the Foreigners' Insularity

America for the Americans! Shelter and welcome let them give to the emigrant and the exile, and make them citizens in so far as civil privileges are concerned. But let it be looked to that paupers and criminals are no longer shipped on us by foreign states. Let it be looked to that foreign nationalities in our midst are rooted out; that foreign regiments and battalions are disarmed; that the public laws and schools of the country are printed and taught in the language of the land; that no more charters for foreign titled or foreign charactered associations—benevolent, social or other—are granted by our legislatures; that all National and State support given to Education, have not the shadow of sectarianism about it. There is work for Americans to do. They have slept on guard—if, indeed, they have been on guard—and the enemy have grown strong and riotous in their midst.

America for the Americans! We have had enough of "Young Irelands," "Young Germanys," and "Young Italys." We have had enough of insolent alien threat to suppress our "Puritan Sabbath," and amend our Constitution. We have been a patient camel, and borne foreign burden even to the back-breaking pound. But the time is come to right the wrong; the occasion is ripe for reform in whatever we have failed. The politico-religious foe is fully discovered; he must be squarely met, and put down. We want in this free land none of this political dictation. . . . Our feeling is earnest, not bitter. The matters of which we have written are great and grave ones, and we shall not be silent until we have aided in wholly securing *America for the Americans!*

Viewpoint 4

"The real American . . . is he . . . who, abandoning every other country and forswearing every other allegiance, gives his mind and heart to the grand constituent ideas of the Republic."

America Has Room for All Loyal Citizens

Putnam's Monthly

Putnam's Monthly was a magazine founded and published by George Putnam from 1853 to 1857. It included articles on politics and the arts by some of America's most famous writers, including Horace Greeley, James Fenimore Cooper, and Henry David Thoreau.

Putnam's Monthly was published during the heyday of the Know-Nothing Party, a political organization whose mission was to severely restrict immigration to the United States. The conservative Know-Nothing Party's motto was "America for Americans." The liberal *Putnam's Monthly* responded to the Know-Nothings with an editorial in 1855, excerpted below, titled "Who Are Americans?" The editors argue that the American institutions of voting and jury trials, among others, are what make people Americans. When foreigners are allowed and encouraged to participate in these institutions, they will no longer consider themselves residents of their former country; they have become Americans. Furthermore, the editors contend, the so-

Putnam's Monthly, "Who Are Americans?" *Putnam's Monthly*, May 1855.

called native Americans are actually immigrants themselves; the only true native Americans are the American Indians who were there when the first immigrants landed. According to the editors, Americans come from the same stock as Europeans and are thus not of a better nature.

What is America, and who are Americans? . . . Accordingly as you answer will the phrase appear very wise or very foolish. If you are determined to consider America as nothing more than the two or three million square miles of dirt included between the Granite Hills and the Pacific, and Americans as those men exclusively whose bodies happened to be fashioned from it, we fear that you have not penetrated to the real beauty and significance of the terms. The soul of a muckworm may very naturally be contented with identifying itself with the mould from which it is bred, and into which it will soon be resolved, but the soul of a man, unless we are hugely misinformed, claims a loftier origin and looks forward to a nobler destiny.

America Is More than a Place

America, in our sense of the word, embraces a complex idea. It means, not simply the soil with its coal, cotton, and corn, but the nationality by which that soil is occupied, and the political system in which such occupants are organized. . . .

America is the democratic republic—not the government of the people by a despot, nor by an oligarchy, nor by any class such as the red-haired part of the inhabitants, or the blue-eyed part; nor yet a government for any other end than the good of the entire nation— but the democratic republic, pure and simple. This is the political organism which individualizes us, or separates us as a living unity from all the rest of the world. All this, of course, would be too elementary to be recounted in any mature discussion, if recent events had not made it necessary to an adequate answer of our second question—who, then, are Americans? Who constitute the people in whose hands the destinies of America are to be deposited?

The fashionable answer in these times is "the natives of this continent, to be sure!" But let us ask again, in that case, whether our old friends Uncas and Chingachgook, and Kag-ne-ga-bow-wow, whether Walk-in-the-water, and Talking-snake, and Big-yellow-thunder, are to be considered Americans par excellence? Alas, no! for they, poor fellows! are all trudging towards the setting sun, and soon their red and dusky figures will have faded in the darker shadows of the night! Is it, then, the second generation of na-tives—they who are driving them away—who compose exclu-sively the American family? You say yes; but we say no! Because, if America be as we have shown, more than the soil of America, we do not see how a mere cloddy derivation from it entitles one to the name of American. . . .

The real American, then, is he . . . who, abandoning every other country and forswearing every other allegiance, gives his mind and heart to the grand constituent ideas of the Republic—to the im-pulses and ends in which and by which alone it subsists. If they have arrived at years of discretion—if he produces evidence of a capacity to understand the relations he undertakes—if he has resided in the atmosphere of freedom long enough to catch its genuine spirit—then is he an American, in the true and best sense of the term.

Or, if not an American, pray what is he? An Englishman, a Ger-man, an Irishman he can no longer be; he has cast off the slough of his old political relations forever; he has asserted his sacred right of expatriation (which the United States was the first of nations to sanction) or been expatriated by his too ardent love of the cause which the United States represents; and he can never return to the ancient fold. It would spurn him more incontinently than pow-der spurns the fire. He must become, then, either a wanderer and a nondescript on the face of the earth, or be received into our gen-erous republican arms. It is our habit to say that we know of no race or creed, but the race of man and the creed of democracy, and if he appeals to us, as a man and a democrat, there is no al-ternative in the premises. We must either deny his claims alto-gether—deny that he is a son of God and our brother—or else we must incorporate him, in due season, into the household. It is not enough that we offer him shelter from the rain—not enough that we mend his looped and windowed raggedness—not enough that we replenish his wasted midriff with bacon and hominy, and open to his palsied hands an opportunity to toil. These are commendable charities, but they are such charities as any one, not himself a brute, would willingly extend to a horse found astray on the common. Shall we do no more for our fellows? . . .

Sentiment Does Not Mean Disloyalty

The adoptive citizen, no doubt, preserves a keen remembrance of his native land; but "lives there on earth a soul so dead" as not to sympathize in that feeling? Let us ask you, oh patriotic Weissnicht, all fresh as you are from the vociferations of the lodge, whether you do at heart think the less of a man because he cannot wholly forget the play-place of his infancy, the friends and companions of his boyhood, the old cabin in which he was reared, and the grave in which the bones of his honored mother repose? Have you never seen two long-separated friends, from the old world, meet again in the new, and clasp each other in a warm embrace, while their conversation blossomed up from a vein of common memory, in "Sweet household talk, and phrases of the hearth," and did you not love them the more, in that their eyes grew liquid with the dear old themes? Or is there, in the whole circle of your large and respectable private acquaintance, a single Scotchman to whom you refuse your hand because his affections melt under the "Auld Lang Syne" of [Robert] Burns, or because his sides shake like a falling house when "Halloween" or "Tam O'Shanter" is read? Can you blame even the poor Frenchman if his eyes light up into a kind of deathless glow when the "Marseillaise," twisted from some wandering hurdy-gurdy, has yet power to recall the glorious days in which his fathers and brothers danced for liberty's sake, and with gay audacity, towards the guillotine? We venture to say for you, No! and we believe, if the truth were told, that often, on the lonely western plains, you have dreamed over again with the German his sweet dream of the resurrection and unity of the Fatherland? We have ourselves seen you, at the St. George dinners, oh Weissnicht, swell with a very evident pride when some flagrant Englishman, recounting, not the battles which his ancestors for ten centuries had won on every field of Europe, but the better trophies gained by [William] Shakespeare, [John] Milton, [Francis]

Bacon, or [Oliver] Cromwell, told you that a little of that same blood coursed in your veins! The blood itself, as it tingled through your body and suffused your cheeks, confessed the fact, if your words did not! How, then, can you, who gaze at Bunker Hill with tears in your eyes, and fling up your hat of a Fourth of July with a jerk that almost dislocates the shoulder, retire to your secret conclave, and chalk it up behind the door, against the foreigner, that he has a lingering love for his native country? Why, he ought to be despised if he had not, if he could forget his heritages of old renown, for it is this traditional tenderness, these genial memories of the immortal words and deeds and places, that constitute his patronymic glories, which show that he has a human heart still under his jacket, and is all the more likely, on account of it, to become a worthy American. . . .

Compare the farmers of our prairies to the boors of the Russian steppes, or to the peasants of the French valleys! Or compare the great body of the working men in England with those of the United States! Now, the American is not of a better nature than the European—for he is often of the same stock—nor is there any charm in our soil and climate unknown to the soil and climate of the other hemisphere; but there is a difference in institutions. Institutions, with us, are made for men, and not men for the institutions. It is the jury, the ballot-box, the free public assemblage, the local committee, the legislative assembly, the place of trust, and as a result of these, the school and the newspaper, which give such a spur to our activities, and endow us with such political competence. The actual responsibilities of civil life are our support and nutriment, and the wings wherewith we fly.

If, consequently, you desire the foreigner to grow into a good citizen, you must subject him to the influences by which good citizens are made. Train him as you are yourselves trained, under the effective tutelage of the regular routine and responsibility of politics. He will never learn to swim by being kept out of the water, anymore than a slave can become a freeman in slavery. He gets used to independence by the practice of it, as the child gets used to walking by walking. It is exercise alone which brings out and improves all sorts of fitnesses—social as well as physical—and the living of any life alone teaches us how it is to be best lived. Nor will any one work for an end in which he and his have no part. They only act for the community who are of the community. Outsiders are always riders. They stand or sit aloof. They have no special call to promote the internal thrift and order, which may get on as it can, for all them. But incorporate them into it, and it is as dear as the apple of their eye.

CHAPTER 2

The Great Wave: The 1880s to 1920s

✸ Chapter Preface

The first wave of immigrants to the United States in the early nineteenth century was from England, Ireland, Germany, Scandinavia, and other northern European countries. Immigration dropped off sharply during the American Civil War (1861–1865), but rapidly increased after the war's end to levels not previously seen. Millions of Italians, Greeks, Russians, Slavs, and other eastern Europeans began arriving en masse. This second major wave of immigrants, known as the "Great Wave," was different from anything Americans had ever seen before, and many Americans feared people from cultures so foreign to them.

Prior to the 1880s, roughly only 10 percent of all immigrants were from Italy, Spain, Greece, Russia, Poland, Hungary, Romania, and other eastern European countries. In 1907, when nearly 1.3 million immigrants arrived in the United States, almost 81 percent were from these countries, and only 19 percent were from England, Ireland, Germany, and Scandinavia.

The immigrants who were part of the Great Wave were different from earlier immigrants in other ways as well. For the most part, the new immigrants were poor, unskilled, illiterate, dark skinned, dark haired, and often Jewish. The governments in their countries of origin were usually absolute monarchies, and these immigrants had little working knowledge of democratic institutions. In addition, for the first time, a large number of immigrants were "birds of passage"—single men who came to the United States to earn their fortunes and then return to their homelands, rather than settling in and building a life and family in America.

Such a change in the ethnic composition, habits, and heritage of immigrants had a profound effect on Americans. Nativism—the belief that "native" inhabitants (who were often themselves immigrants or children of immigrants) were better Americans than immigrants—made a brief resurgence. Unlike during other periods of nativism in which anti-immigrant hostility was directed at specific groups such as the Irish, this time all immigrants were the focus of nativist feelings.

In response to native fears about these new immigrants, the government tried to change the newcomers' culture, values, and especially their language. The U.S. Bureau of Americanization encouraged employers to make their foreign-born workers take compulsory English classes. Many jurisdictions prohibited schools from teaching in any language other than English, and some elementary schools even banned the teaching of foreign languages.

Americans feared other things about the new immigrants besides their language and values. Many labor leaders believed that the wages and jobs of native workers were threatened by the new immigrants, who were willing to work for lower wages than Americans. In fact, they believed that American companies were importing these foreigners specifically for that reason. In addition, many Americans believed that the Catholic Church—with the help of Catholic immigrants—was plotting to overthrow the American government. And because many Russian immigrants active in the labor movement were radicals and anarchists, Americans believed that these foreigners were dangerous and posed a serious threat to the United States. The Italian immigrants became associated with organized crime and blood feuds, with many unsolved murders laid at their feet. Jews were the object of suspicion and dislike because of their long beards, strange clothing, rigid religious observances, and the unfamiliar markings of their Yiddish shop signs. For these reasons and others, Americans came to see the new immigrants as the "scum of Europe."

During the Great Wave of immigration, many Americans began to argue loudly for limits on who should be allowed to immigrate to the United States, and indeed, it was during this period that the first restrictions were put in place. However, it was also during this period that many Americans came to see their country as one that welcomed the "huddled masses yearning to be free." The authors in the following chapter discuss the conflict between these two views of immigration during the Great Wave.

Viewpoint 1

"All the good the United States could do by offering indiscriminate hospitality to a few millions more of European peasants . . . would not compensate for any permanent injury done to our republic."

The New Immigrants Harm American Society

Francis A. Walker

Francis A. Walker was an economics professor at Yale University, the president of Massachusetts Institute of Technology, and president of the American Statistical Association and the American Economic Association in the late nineteenth century. In the following viewpoint, Walker contends that although immigrants who arrived in the United States during the first half of the 1800s benefited the young country, immigrants who arrived during the second half of the nineteenth century have become a burden. America no longer has the open land for immigrants to settle. The prices for agricultural goods have fallen, thereby reducing the farmers' ability to pay for unskilled immigrant labor to sow and harvest the crops. Unemployment has also become a serious problem across the country, he asserts, for skilled and unskilled workers alike. But perhaps the biggest threat of all,

Francis A. Walker, "Restriction of Immigration," *Atlantic Monthly*, June 1896.

Walker argues, is that the new immigrants—who come from southern Italy, Hungary, Austria, and Russia—are unskilled workers who lack the character and industry to become upstanding American citizens. Therefore, he concludes, in order to protect the United States against these hordes of European peasants, immigration should be restricted.

L et us now inquire what are the changes in our general conditions which seem to demand a revision of the opinion and policy heretofore held regarding immigration. Three of these are subjective, affecting our capability of easily and safely taking care of a large and tumultuous access of foreigners; the fourth is objective, and concerns the character of the immigration now directed upon our shores. Time will serve for only a rapid characterization.

First, we have the important fact of the complete exhaustion of the free public lands of the United States. Fifty years ago, thirty years ago, vast tracts of arable land were open to every person arriving on our shores, under the Preemption Act, or later, the Homestead Act. A good farm of one hundred and sixty acres could be had at the minimum price of $1.25 an acre, or for merely the fees of registration. Under these circumstances it was a very simple matter to dispose of a large immigration. To-day there is not a good farm within the limits of the United States which is to be had under either of these acts. The wild and tumultuous scenes which attended the opening to settlement of the Territory of Oklahoma, a few years ago, and, a little later, of the so-called Cherokee Strip, testify eloquently to the vast change in our national conditions in this respect. This is not to say that more people cannot and will not, sooner or later, with more or less of care and pains and effort, be placed upon the land of the United States; but it does of itself alone show how vastly the difficulty of providing for immigration has increased. The immigrant must now buy his farm from a second hand, and he must pay the price which the value of the land for agricultural purposes determines. In the case of ninety-five out of a hundred immigrants, this necessity puts an immediate occupation of the soil out of the question.

A second change in our national condition, which importantly affects our capability of taking care of large numbers of ignorant and unskilled foreigners, is the fall of agricultural prices which has gone on steadily since 1873. It is not of the slightest consequence to inquire into the causes of this fall, whether we refer it to the competition of Argentina and of India or the appreciation of gold. We are interested only in the fact. There has been a great reduction in the cost of producing crops in some favored regions where steam-ploughs and steam-reaping, steam-threshing, and steam-sacking machines can be employed; but there has been no reduction in the cost of producing crops upon the ordinary American farm at all corresponding to the reduction in the price of the produce. It is a necessary consequence of this that the ability to employ a large number of uneducated and unskilled hands in agriculture has greatly diminished.

A Labor Problem

Still a third cause which may be indicated, perhaps more important than either of those thus far mentioned, is found in the fact that we have now a labor problem.` We in the United States have been wont to pride ourselves greatly upon our so easily maintaining peace and keeping the social order unimpaired. We have, partly from a reasonable patriotic pride, partly also from something like Phariseeism, been much given to pointing at our European cousins, and boasting superiority over them in this respect. Our self-gratulation has been largely due to overlooking social differences between us and them. That boasted superiority has been owing mainly, not to our institutions, but to our more favorable conditions. There is no country of Europe which has not for a long time had a labor problem; that is, which has not so largely exploited its own natural resources, and which has not a labor supply so nearly meeting the demands of the market at their fullest, that hard times and periods of industrial depression have brought a serious strain through extensive non-employment of labor. From this evil condition we have, until recently, happily been free. During the last few years, however, we have ourselves come under the shadow of this evil, in spite of our magnificent natural resources. We know what it is to have even intelligent and skilled labor unemployed through considerable periods of time. This change of conditions is likely to bring some abatement to our national pride. No longer is it a matter of course that every industrious and temperate man can find work in the United States. And it is to be remembered that, of all nations, we are the one which is least qualified to deal with a labor problem. We have not the machinery, we have not the army, we have not the police, we have not the traditions and instincts, for dealing with such a matter, as the great railroad and other strikes of the last few years have shown.

The Average Immigrant Has Changed

I have spoken of three changes in the national condition, all subjective, which greatly affect our capability of dealing with a large and tumultuous immigration. There is a fourth, which is objective. It concerns the character of the foreigners now resorting to our shores. Fifty, even thirty years ago, there was a rightful presumption regarding the average immigrant that he was among the most enterprising, thrifty, alert, adventurous, and courageous of the community from which he came. It required no small energy, prudence, forethought, and pains to conduct the inquiries relating to his migration, to accumulate the necessary means, and to find his way across the Atlantic. To-day the presumption is completely reversed. So thoroughly has the continent of Europe been crossed by railways, so effectively has the business of emigration there been exploited, so much have the rates of railroad fares and ocean passage been reduced, that it is now among the least thrifty and prosperous members of any European community that the emigration agent finds his best recruiting-ground. The care and pains required have been reduced to a minimum, while the agent of the Red Star Line or the White Star Line is everywhere at hand, to suggest migration to those who are not getting on well at home. The intending emigrants are looked after from the moment they are locked into the cars in their native villages until they stretch themselves upon the floors of the buildings on Ellis Island, in New York. Illustrations of the ease and facility with which this Pipe Line Immigration is now carried on might be given in profusion. So broad and smooth is the channel, there is no reason why every foul and stagnant pool of population in Europe, which no breath of intellectual or industrial life has stirred for ages, should not be decanted upon our soil. Hard times here may momentarily check the flow; but it will not be permanently stopped so long as *any difference of economic level* exists between our population and that of the most degraded communities abroad.

The New Immigrant

But it is not alone that the presumption regarding the immigrant of to-day is so widely different from that which existed regarding the immigrant of thirty or fifty years ago. The immigrant of the former time came almost exclusively from western and northern Europe. We have now tapped great reservoirs of population then almost unknown to the passenger lists of our arriving vessels. Only a short time ago, the immigrants from southern Italy, Hungary, Austria, and Russia together made up hardly more than one per cent of our immigration. To-day the proportion has risen to something like forty per cent, and threatens soon to become fifty or sixty per cent, or even more. The entrance into our political, social, and industrial life of such vast masses of peasantry, degraded below our utmost conceptions, is a matter which no intelligent patriot can look upon without the gravest apprehension and alarm. These people have no history behind them which is of a nature to give encouragement. They have none of the inherited instincts and tendencies which made it comparatively easy to deal with the immigration of the olden time. They are beaten men from beaten races; representing the worst failures in the struggle for existence. . . .

Their habits of life, again, are of the most revolting kind. Read the description given by Mr. [Jacob] Riis [in *How the Other Half Lives*] of the police driving from the garbage dumps the miserable beings who try to burrow in those depths of unutterable filth and slime in order that they may eat and sleep there! Was it in cement like this that the foundations of our republic were laid? What effects must be produced upon our social standards, and upon the ambitions and aspirations of our people, by a contact so foul and loathsome? The influence upon the American rate of wages of a competition like this cannot fail to be injurious and even disastrous. Already it has been seriously felt in the tobacco manufacture, in the clothing trade, and in many forms of mining industry; and unless this access of vast numbers of unskilled workmen of the lowest type, in a market already fully supplied with labor, shall be checked, it cannot fail to go on from bad to worse, in breaking down the standard which has been maintained with so much care and at so much cost. The competition of paupers is far more telling and more killing than the competition of pauper-made goods. Degraded labor in the slums of foreign cities may be prejudicial to intelligent, ambitious, self-respecting labor here; but it does not threaten half so much evil as does degraded labor in the garrets of our native cities.

A Menace to Political Safety

Finally, the present situation is most menacing to our peace and political safety. In all the social and industrial disorders of this country since 1877, the foreign elements have proved themselves the ready tools of demagogues in defying the law, in destroying property, and in working violence. A learned clergyman who mingled with the socialistic mob which, two years ago, threatened the State House and the governor of Massachusetts, told me that during the entire disturbance he heard no word spoken in any language which he knew,—either in English, in German, or in French. There may be those who can contemplate the addition to our population of vast numbers of persons having no inherited instincts of self-government and respect for law; knowing no restraint upon their own passions but the club of the policeman or the bayonet of the soldier; forming communities, by the tens of thousands, in which only foreign tongues are spoken, and into which can steal no influence from our free institutions and from popular discussion. But I confess to being far less optimistic. I have conversed with one of the highest officers of the United States army and with one of the highest officers of the civil government regarding the state of affairs which existed during the summer of 1894; and the revelations they made of facts not generally known, going to show how the ship of state grazed along its whole side upon the rocks, were enough to appall the most sanguine American, the most hearty believer in free government. Have we the right to expose the republic to any increase of the dangers from this source which now so manifestly threaten our peace and safety?

The First Law of Nature

For it is never to be forgotten that self-defense is the first law of nature and of nations. If that man who careth not for his own household is worse than an infidel, the nation which permits its institutions to be endangered by any cause which can fairly be removed is guilty not leas in Christian than in natural law. Charity begins at home; and while the people of the United States have gladly offered an asylum to millions upon millions of the distressed and unfortunate of other lands and climes, they have no right to carry their hospitality one step beyond the line where American institutions, the American rate of wages, the American standard of living, are brought into serious peril. All the good the United States could do by offering indiscriminate hospitality to a few millions more of European peasants, whose places at home will, within another generation, be filled by others as miserable as themselves, would not compensate for any permanent injury done to our republic. Our highest duty to charity and to humanity is to make this great experiment, here, of free laws and educated labor, the most triumphant success that can possibly be attained. In this way we shall do far more for Europe than by allowing its city slums and its vast stagnant reservoirs of degraded peasantry to be drained off upon our soil. Within the decade between 1880 and 1890 five and a quarter millions of foreigners entered our ports! No nation in human history ever undertook to deal with such masses of alien population. That man must be a sentimentalist and an optimist beyond all bounds of reason who believes that we can take such a load upon the national stomach without a failure of assimilation, and without great danger to the health and life of the nation. For one, I believe it is time that we should take a rest, and give our social, political, and industrial system some chance to recuperate. The problems which so sternly confront us to-day are serious enough without being complicated and aggravated by the addition of some millions of Hungarians, Bohemians, Poles, south Italians, and Russian Jews.

Viewpoint 2

"Our powers as a nation and our prosperity as individuals would only have been a fraction of what they are had immigration been prevented."

The New Immigrants Benefit American Society

A. Piatt Andrew

A. Piatt Andrew, a congressman from Massachusetts, discounts the fears of anti-immigrationists who claim that new immigrants harm American society. Writing in the June 1914 issue of the *North American Review*, he points out that Americans have always feared the impact of immigrants on American society, and those fears have always been groundless. In the early nineteenth century, for example, many Americans were certain that the large influx of Irish immigrants would cause America to crumble. Instead, the Irish became mainstays of the labor market and influential in politics and other areas of American life.

In the following excerpt, Andrew maintains that the Immigration Commission's massive study of immigrants, researched between 1907 and 1910 and resulting in a forty-one-volume report, turned up no hard evidence of inferiority on the part of

A. Piatt Andrew, *North American Review*, June 1914.

the new immigrants in the areas of health, crime, and dependency on social welfare. He argues that the educational and economic opportunities offered by the United States soon turn rough immigrants into productive members of society.

Andrew was a professor of economics at Harvard University and an expert assistant and editor of publications at the National Monetary Commission. He also served as director of the U.S. Mint, secretary of the U.S. Treasury, and treasurer of the American Red Cross.

The subject of immigration we have always with us in this country. It has been a topic of contentious interest and legislation almost continuously since the first Englishman set foot in the Western World. The Pilgrims and Puritans of Massachusetts Bay were scarcely settled in their log huts before they began planning a policy of exclusion, and already in 1637 they voted to keep out those who were not members of their own religious sect. So in the very earliest decades of the English settlement, immigration began to be restricted, and Quakers and Baptists, Episcopalians and Catholics, were banished and proscribed from the Commonwealth on the ground that American standards were apt to be impaired by their admission. From that day to this the older immigrants and their descendants have tried to keep this country for those already here and their kindred folk. They have looked upon themselves as a kind of aristocracy, their supposed superiority being proportioned to the length of time that they and their ancestors have lived upon this continent, and each successive generation of immigrants newly arrived has tended with curious repetition to adopt the same viewpoint, to believe that the succeeding immigrants were inferior to the former in religion, habits, education, or what not, and ought to be kept out. Then for more than a hundred years a further motive for exclusion has found constant iteration. Each generation has been taught to believe that the country was rapidly filling to the brim, and that on that account also the doors of entry ought to be closed.

In the very first decade of our Federal Government, in 1797, when the first Alien Act was under consideration, we find passages

in the records of Congress which sound much like utterances of
certain Congressmen in 1914:

> When the country, said Otis (in 1797), was new it may have
> been good policy to admit all. But it is so no longer. A bar
> should be placed against the admittance of those restless
> people who cannot be tranquil and happy at home. We do
> not want a vast horde of wild Irishmen let loose upon us.

Passage after passage of similar tenor could be cited from every
subsequent decade, but I shall only quote one or two examples,
beginning with a report made in 1819 by the Managers of the Society for the Prevention of Pauperism in the City of New York. In
this report [by the Industrial Commission] of nearly a hundred
years ago the fear is expressed that through immigration

> pauperism threatens us with the most overwhelming conse-
> quences. . . . The present state of Europe contributes in a thou-
> sand ways to foster increasing immigration to the United States.
> . . . An almost innumerable population beyond the ocean is out
> of employment. . . . This country is the resort of vast numbers
> of these needy and wretched beings. . . . They are frequently
> found destitute in our streets: they seek employment at our
> doors: they are found in our almshouses and in our hospitals:
> they are found at the bar of our criminal tribunals, in our
> bridewell and our penitentiary and our State prison.

This was in 1819. Coming down another score of years, we find
the next generation once more extolling the immigration up to its
own time, but once more greatly perturbed by the supposedly inferior character of the immigrants then beginning to come. In a
paper [on the Hearings before the Committee on Immigration of
the Sixty-First Congress] published in 1835, entitled "Imminent
Dangers to the Institutions of the United States through Foreign
Immigration, we read that formerly

> our accessions of immigration were real accessions of strength
> from the ranks of the learned and the good, from enlightened
> mechanic and artisan and intelligent husbandmen. Now im-
> migration is the accession of weakness, from the ignorant and

vicious, or the priest-ridden slaves of Ireland and Germany, or the outcast tenants of the poorhouses and prisons of Europe.

In the course of the twenty years that followed came the great increase of Irish immigrants during the famine in Ireland, and then again many Americans became panic-stricken at the thought of the possible consequences. A great secret order and a new political party, the so-called Know-Nothings, were organized to overcome the dire results that were apprehended. The abject squalor and wretchedness to which these Irish immigrants had for generations been accustomed, it was urged, could not but result in the degradation of American standards, and many seemed to fear that on account of their religion the immigrants would try to overthrow our democratic government and establish an ecclesiastic hierarchy in its stead. Feeling in some places was so bitter that the immigrants were mobbed in the streets, their churches were desecrated, and their children were persecuted in the public schools. One could spend hours reading passages from speeches and pamphlets of this period denouncing the Irish immigration.

Yet the American government still lives and, notwithstanding the abject condition of these Irish settlers and the fears and apprehensions which they aroused, we have absorbed and assimilated some four millions of them and no one has yet observed any deterioration of American standards and ideals in consequence. We and they have flourished and prospered, and we reckon their descendants among our best citizens. The names of many of them are daily on our lips and before our eyes in the headlines, for they are our political magnates, our aldermen and mayors and governors.

Passing on to the next generation, during the later seventies and early eighties came a great migration of Germans and Scandinavians, and once more racial prejudice found a new objective. The previous immigrants had for the most part spoken our language, were akin, it was said, to our original stock and familiar with our traditions, but the new immigrants, ignorant of English and with different modes of thought and practice, were held to be unassimilable and to menace our standards and institutions. The apprehension was so great and the objection became so general as to induce in 1882 the first general immigration law. Nevertheless, we have absorbed over four million Germans and over two million Swedes and Norwegians, and to-day we count no more valuable factors in our national stock than their descendants.

The New Immigrants

But once again the racial currents shifted, and during the last fifteen years new vast streams have flowed to this country from Russia, Italy, and Austria-Hungary, and new smaller streams from Portugal and from Greece, Rumania, and other parts of Eastern Europe. During 1913 Russia, Italy, and Austria-Hungary offered each nearly a quarter of the year's total inflow. So once again the familiar clamor of alarm has been turned in another direction. It is now admitted that the millions of Irish and Germans and Scandinavians who have come into the country have been absorbed without any degradation of our standards, that they have rendered invaluable service in developing the country, and that the earlier fears have proven groundless. But it is said that the new immigrant is of a type radically less desirable than that of the earlier periods, and once more we hear the warning that the situation to-day is different in that the country is now thickly settled and land and opportunities are no longer available. As I recall the similar assertions and fears of earlier periods I must confess that I sympathize with the gentleman from Missouri who expressed a desire to have some evidence submitted. It looks as if in the eyes of some Americans the only good immigrants were the dead immigrants, and that the only opportunities for the country's development lay in the past. I want to know and you want to know in what sense the immigrants of to-day are thought to be inferior to those who preceded them, and on what grounds it is claimed that the country has reached the limit of profitable increase in population.

Are the new immigrants less sound of body and mind than those of earlier generations? Do they more frequently evince criminal proclivities? Are they more apt to become a charge upon the State? Is their standard of living lower? Are they less capable of becoming loyal, worthy American citizens? We may well inquire what the Immigration Commission, with their exhaustive investigations published in forty-one volumes, have to say in answer to these questions, and in this connection we may also turn to the volume upon *The Immigration Problem* prepared by Professors Jenks and Lauck, the reputed authors of the Immigration Commission Report, which summarizes the data and conclusions of the Commission.

Are the new immigrants wanting in bodily vigor and health? The authors of the Immigration Commission Report deny this.

Our later immigration laws have forbidden the entrance of those afflicted with any loathsome or contagious disease, or of those in such a condition of health as is likely to make them become a public charge. Under these laws, too, the steamship companies are held responsible and are compelled to return free of charge passengers rejected by our immigration officials, and in the case of the insane or diseased they are fined in addition one hundred dollars for each such passenger brought to this country. This legislation has brought about a very great change in the matter of inspection and exclusion, and the representatives of the Immigration Commission declare that

> the careful inspection abroad, sometimes by representatives of the United States Government, otherwise by inspectors of the steamship companies, and the final examination at the port of entry, have brought about the result that with very rare exceptions every immigrant admitted to this country is now in good health, and is not bringing with him the germs of any disease that might prove detrimental.

And they add that

> as far as one can judge from the records kept, the races of the recent immigration, those from Southern and Eastern Europe, are not so subject to diseases that seem to be allied with moral weaknesses as some of those of the older immigration races.

Are the new immigrants more addicted to crime? Again the authors of the Immigration Commission Report assert that there is no proof of this.

> No satisfactory evidence has yet been produced to show that immigration has resulted in an increase in crime disproportionate to the increase in the adult population. Such compa-

rable statistics of crime and population as it has been possible to obtain indicate that immigrants are less prone to commit crime than are native Americans.

Are the new immigrants more likely to become charges upon the community? The authors of the Immigration Commission Report declare the contrary.

The Immigration Commission, with the assistance of the Associated Charities in forty-three cities, including practically all the large centers excepting New York, reached the conclusion that only a very small percentage of the immigrants now arriving apply for relief.

Is the standard of living of the new immigrants lower than that of the old? Any one who has read the contemporary descriptions of the living conditions of the Irish and German immigrants in the periods from 1840 to 1880 will hesitate to believe that the standard of living of the immigrants of our day is lower than the standard of living of the immigrants in the earlier period. Nothing could be more pitiful and depressing than the pictures of the poverty and wretchedness of the Irish settlers at the time of the great migration from Ireland. The majority of the Irish people for centuries had been forced to live in hovels with only the barest necessities in the way of furniture and clothing, and many of the thousands who came to this country were in serious danger of actual starvation if they remained at home. The authors of the Immigration Commission Report state that "practically none of our immigrants of the present day are in such a condition."

In a very few years, with our free and compulsory schools, our free libraries, and the economic opportunities which this country has to offer, these people were transformed into ambitious, self-respecting, public-spirited citizens. And so it is with the Italians and Poles, the Russian Jews, and other poor immigrants of more recent times. They are often very poor in this world's goods when they enter our gates. One sees the mothers coming in with shawls in place of hats, often without shoes or stockings, and with all their worldly belongings in a rough box or tied in a single handkerchief. But it is one of the miraculous phases of our history how quickly we are able to transform, enrich, and absorb them. A few years later one sees the children of these same immigrants well dressed and ambitious, well educated, and literally undistinguishable in manners, morals, or appearance from the descendants of those who came over in the *Mayflower*. Such is the Aladdin-like power of the great American melting-pot.

It is easy to echo the cry of prejudice if you happen to be of Anglo-Saxon descent, and to assume an air of superiority and denounce the Italians, Greeks, Poles, Bohemians, and Russian Jews, as if they ranked somewhere between man and the beast, but were not yet wholly human. The same intolerant attitude of mind among the Anglo-Saxon Puritan settlers of early colonial days led to the whipping, imprisonment, banishment, and even hanging of Quakers and others of unlike religious beliefs. If you share these prejudices to-day, walk some Sunday afternoon through the galleries of the art-museums in our large cities and note who are the people most interested in their treasures; inquire at the public libraries who are their most appreciative patrons; visit the night schools and observe who constitute their most eager classes; study the lineage of the ranking students in our universities and you will find that our libraries, art-galleries, universities, and schools often find their best patrons among the offspring of these despised races of Southern and Eastern Europe. Or if you seek your information in books, I would commend you to authorities who have studied the new immigrants at first-hand. If you will examine the volume on *The Italian in America*, by Messrs. Lord, Trenor, and Barrows, you will be reminded of what America owes to the Italians from Columbus down to our own day. And if you will read the study of *Our Slavic Fellow-Citizen*, by Dr. Balch, you will be reminded of what we owe to the Poles and Bohemians from the time of [Casimir] Pulaski [Polish commander of the American cavalry during the American war of independence] and [Tadeusz] Kosciuszko [Polish hero of American war of independence] down to our time. And if you will read the story of *The Promised Land* and *They Who Knock at Our Gates*, by Mary Antin, you will find descriptions of what we may expect from the Russian Jews. Incidentally you will also discover that the traditions and heroes of American history find their most ardent admirers to-day among these same people who but recently were aliens.

There is no evidence that the newer immigrants are inferior to the old. It is only the recurrence of a groundless prejudice which makes some people feel so. But even if the new immigration is not inferior in character to the old, we have still to ask whether there is not a menace in the very numbers of the immigrants now coming in. We hear a great deal these days about the alarming increase in immigration. We are told that more than a million foreign-born are coming into this country every year, that the number is increasing as never before, and that the country cannot absorb so great an influx. What are the facts in this regard?

As to the amount of recent immigration, the tide ebbs and flows with the alternating advances and recessions of business, and the tendency is for each successive wave to reach a higher level than its predecessors. In 1854 a record of 428,000 arrivals was established; then there was a great recession, and in 1873 a new high level of 460,000 was reached. The next wave culminated in 1882 with 789,000, and in 1907 the highest of all immigrant records was reached, 1,285,000. During the last ten years the average number of immigrants arriving in this country has not fallen much short of a million per year, and this figure considered by itself does look portentous. One must bear in mind, however, that it represents only one side of the ledger and is subject to very heavy deductions. If you are reckoning the extent to which your property has increased during a given period, it does not suffice merely to count up the income. You must also deduct the outgo. And if you are reckoning the actual addition to our population which results from immigration, if you would have in mind the actual number of immigrants that we have had to absorb, you must take account of both sides of the ledger, of the outgo as well as of the income. During the last six years the number of departing aliens has been carefully collated, and it appears that from 400,000 to 700,000 aliens depart from the United States every year. This leaves a net balance of arriving aliens of only about 550,000 per year, or only about one-half of the total that is commonly cited as representing the annual influx. Even this figure may look precarious, however, until we have considered it in its appropriate relations and comparisons.

America's Capacity

The capacity of the country to assimilate the incoming thousands without any serious modification of our institutions or standards depends in part upon two conditions: first, upon the proportion which the aliens bear to the resident population by which they are to be absorbed, and, second, upon whether the country is already approaching the saturation point as regards the density of its population. Now the proportion of foreign-born in our total population has not varied much in recent decades, and even in the record year of 1907 the percentage of immigrants to population was lower than it has been on several other occasions during the past sixty years. As compared with the population of the country the immigration of recent years has not bulked as large as the immigration of the early fifties, and if we consider only the net immigration, it makes to-day an addition to the total population of the country of only a little more than one-half of one per cent. per year.

Nor need one fear that we are reaching the point in this country where population presses upon the means of subsistence. The number of our people will have to be multiplied sixfold to equal the density of the population of France, to be multiplied tenfold to equal that of Germany or that of Italy, and to be multiplied eighteenfold to equal that of England. If the present population of the whole United States were located in the State of Texas alone, there would still not be two-thirds as many inhabitants per square mile in that State as there are to-day in England. One must, indeed, have little faith in the future of the United States who, in the face of such comparisons, believes that the population of this country as a whole is approaching the saturation point, or that from the standpoint of the country as a whole we need be terrified by the dimensions of present immigration. It amounts in annual net to little more than one-half of one per cent. of our present population, and that population will have to increase many hundred per cent. before we have reached a density remotely approaching that of any of the leading countries of Europe.

There will, of course, always be timid Americans who will wonder how we can possibly hope to assimilate foreigners to the extent of as much as one-half of one per cent. of our population per year and who would prefer to see the country relatively weak and undeveloped than run the risk of continuing the experiment. When Jefferson proposed to purchase all of the great territory west of the Mississippi known as Louisiana, the citizens of Boston organized a public meeting to protest against the project. They thought it would destroy the relative influence of New England in the country's affairs, and they thought that the United States could not assimilate so vast a territory; and though their fears have been proven not only groundless but absurd by subsequent history, there are many still in Boston and elsewhere in the country who feel that our powers of assimilation have now reached their limit of capacity and ought not to be further taxed.

There will, of course, always be Americans absorbed in history and genealogy who will sigh for the good old days when America was only a sparsely settled fringe of seaboard States, and who will wish that the population of the country might still consist of the Sons and Daughters of the Revolution, the Colonial Dames, and the Sons of Colonial Wars. This might, indeed, have been a pleasant condition from certain points of view, but of one thing we may be certain: this country to-day would not be settled from coast to coast; our cities would not be a fifth of their present size; our powers as a nation and our prosperity as individuals would only have been a fraction of what they are had immigration been prevented.

Viewpoint 3

"There is not an evil thing among us, not a vice, nor crime, nor disturbing element, which is not for the most part of foreign origin."

Immigration Should Be Restricted

T.T. Munger

The number of immigrants arriving in the United States soared to unprecedented levels during the 1880s. A large majority of these new immigrants were from southern and eastern Europe, areas that had not sent many immigrants to America previously. Many Americans became alarmed at the large number of foreigners who were very different in dress, languages spoken, and culture from U.S. citizens who were white, Anglo-Saxon, and Protestant.

T.T. Munger, a priest who lived in New Haven, Connecticut at the end of the nineteenth century, believes that this new wave of immigrants is composed largely of beggars, criminals, and people otherwise physically, morally, and politically unfit to become Americans. In addition, many immigrants become insane during their trip due to the difficulty of the venture. Munger argues in the following viewpoint that Congress should pass legislation to exclude those immigrants who would not harmoniously fit in to American life. He also recommends that immigrants be required to obtain a passport prior to their arrival; in this way, he argues, the unfit can be screened and

T.T. Munger, "Immigration by Passport," *Century*, March 1888.

weeded out by U.S. officials before they make the arduous journey overseas.

The statistics of foreign immigration and the sources of it are so well known that they scarcely need mention. In the last thirty years, seven and a half millions of immigrants have come to us,— a considerable fraction of the present population. They and their children number fifteen millions, or one-fourth of the people. During the decade ending in 1884 the immigration numbered about four millions. Much of this is in the same racial line with our own—English, Teutonic, and Scandinavian—and so far as blood goes reenforces the national type. But whatever is gained in this respect is more than offset by the blacks, and the mixed Spanish and Indian populations of the South-west, so that we still have from ten to fifteen millions utterly alien to our stock, and for the most part unfit for citizenship. Generalizing these statistics, we have the grave fact that one-fifth of our population is either of blood outside of the national strain or defective in political capacity.

The Foreign Element Is Deteriorating

It now costs thirty dollars or less to transport a Bohemian or Italian from his home to our ports, and five dollars more will place him in the middle of the continent. Absolute paupers cannot make this journey, and there are laws shutting them out, the only penalty of which is the trouble of taking back those who may be detected as paupers or insane. The feebleness of the legislation is exceeded by the weakness of its enforcement. Consequently, we are already burdened with a large element of European paupers and insane. Our beggars are nearly all foreigners, and nearly one-third of our insane are immigrants. . . . This proneness to insanity among immigrants reveals their worn-out vitality, their ignorance, and their inability to endure so great a change; it is the protest of nature against it. But there is a class just above that of the pauper, and into which it is constantly slipping, hardly more desirable, which now avails itself of this cheap transportation. The foreign element is not only increasing, but it is deteriorating. It is beneath the dignity of argument to contend that much of the immigration from Southern and Central Europe, and some also of that from England and Ireland, is unfit, on physical, moral, and political grounds, for incorporation into American life. It is equally beyond dispute that it constitutes a large factor in labor troubles, crowding the market and depressing wages below the American living point. Mr. Carroll D. Wright, in his first annual report as Commissioner of Labor, tells us that already 31.9 per cent. of our mechanical laborers are immigrants, and, while recognizing their value in some respects, finds in the fact a main cause of overproduction and excessive competition. His wise inference is that this immigration should be restricted for the sake of a sound industry. Equally weighty considerations of a political and moral nature could be urged. Baneful as the process and the degree of it are, it seems likely to go on in geometrical ratio. Larger and swifter ships, cheaper railway transportation, the crowding out in Europe, its military laws, the increasing attractions on this continent, and especially the fact that overproduction here through immigration reacts on the labor market there,—such are the forces that swell the current. Thus, the greater the immigration the faster will it increase, and without possibility of end till the balance in populations and resources is reached, and America becomes, in one brief, rapid rush of changing population, another Europe,—a work which, if done at all, should fill centuries. Europe is steady and strong, so far as it is so, because there are behind it two thousand years of consolidating life packed full of binding tradition and usage. We have no past, no traditions, no usage, but only some sound principles of government upon which we rely to do the work of history. We propose to convert and transform the basest populations of the civilized world by the Constitution,—the caucus and the ballot being the nominal teachers, though the real ones are the saloon and the ward politician. Locomotion may be increased to an untold degree, but not the paces of life. Neither the stature of the body nor the growth of the nation can be hastened. We have a population, such as it is, but it is an open question if we have a true nation, or can have one until we take more pains to secure its proper elements. We successfully played the part of the leaven for a long time, but the meal is now not only increasing beyond all measure, but is of a character not to be leavened. The principle of exclusion already recognized in our laws should be made to embrace any element which is not already well fitted to enter harmoniously into the life of the nation. Such legislation would, of course, shock the traditional American sentiment, but there are some things this nation sadly needs to learn if it would remain true to itself; such as courage to resist the clamor of sentimental religionists, political idealists, and atheistic anarchists. These unconsciously play into one another's hands, paralyze parties by their converging streams of talk, and prevent the adoption of any strong, intelligent, and patriotic action. When a board of health was first established in London, Charles Kingsley prayed God that they might be saved from "Idealism." The most homely, practical, unsentimental people in the world, we are yet the most given to following a vague and general idealism. We regulate the details of private life by the severest common sense, but leave great matters of public interest to be settled by what we call *principles.* Reasons for this may be found in our history and in the better parts of human nature, but none the less do they prevent us from drifting into a political life that is without order or reason or purpose.

Foreign Criminals

There is nothing which calls more loudly for a closer restriction of immigration than the inroad of criminals from Europe. Like the first murderer, the criminal is a wanderer; and this being a free country and full of chances, he naturally wanders hither. Seventy-five per cent. of the crime in New England is committed by foreigners. Seventy-four per cent. of the discharged Irish convicts come to this country. It is a common practice of the Irish courts to discharge those accused of crime with the understanding that they shall go to America, and the same thing is done in Switzerland. There are laws against the landing of convicts, but none against accused criminals; still, it is doubtful if one class is hindered more than the other. The hunted anarchists and fugitive nihilists of course come hither, and amuse themselves by publishing treasonable journals and scattering bombs among the police.

The passage of a discharged criminal from one country to another cannot in individual cases be prevented by ordinary legislation, but when there is an immigration of masses of criminals, and the fact enters into the administration of foreign courts of justice, some extraordinary legislation would seem to be necessary. These imported criminals keep our saloons, whence they dictate our politics; they rob our houses, murder us on the street, and crowd our prisons. The time has come when it is not amiss for the American sociologist to fix his eye upon this word *foreign* and measure its import in our social and political life. There is not an evil thing among us, not a vice, nor crime, nor disturbing element, which is not for the most part of foreign origin. Mobs, murder, burglary, ruffianism, boycottism, drunkenness, lawlessness, atheism, bribery, anarchism, political corruption and intrigue,—it is a simple fact that the largest element in each member of this fearful category is mainly composed of foreigners. There are Americans who are criminals, but it can hardly be said that there is an American criminal class.

There is, of course, a worthy and decent immigration, the continuance of which we may invite and even covet; but it should be under restrictions that are effective, and that sharply discriminate against criminals, paupers, insane, Mormons, anarchists, and also against those classes whose depraved social condition renders them unfit to assume the duties of American citizenship. Only the last point is controverted on the ground that it shuts out the ignorant who may become intelligent, the poor who may prove industrious, and that it is a policy essentially inhuman. Such considerations deserve respectful treatment.

Moral Duty

It is urged that it is not just and merciful to close our ports against the poor, the ignorant, the oppressed, and the debased of other lands. It may not be easy to distinguish between the moral duty of the individual and of the nation, so close is the analogy between them; but it is clear that one may do some things as an individual which one may not do as the head of a family, some things as the father of a household which he may not as a citizen. The welfare or safety of others comes in to limit his action and shut it off from what it might be his duty to risk or endure as an individual. If the house of [nineteenth-century French novelist] Victor Hugo's good bishop had held a wife and children, it would not have been right for him to open his doors to Jean Valjean [a character in his *Les Miserables*]; something more than the spoons would have been endangered. The law of mercy and humanity which justifies a man in taking his life in his hand and encountering the last degree of risk and sacrifice does not require him to drag others along his path. It is not asserted that a nation should not be merciful and humane, nor that there are two kinds of morality, but only that the enforcement of even the highest principles has limitations that become moral standards. A corporate body cannot go so fast and so far in sacrificial ways as an individual. The spirit of humanity and mercy is to be always cherished by political bodies, but the degree of its enforcement should be regulated and determined by inseparable circumstances. The head of man may touch the stars, but his feet rest on the dust of the earth. . . .

Immigrants Must Be Fit

It is not a slight thing for a man to change continents, language, citizenship, institutions, customs, hereditary surroundings, and present ties and throw himself into an environment new in every respect save the sky above him. Such an act should be made difficult, so that men shall not rashly undertake it, and it should be suffered only on the ground of entire fitness. The most fit are those whose intelligence renders them least dependent upon environment; and the least fit are those who are still the creatures of environment. Immigration is largely tragical, as is shown by the statistics of insanity. The ratio of insane foreigners to native born is about three to one; of those born of foreign parents to native born, nearly four to one. These facts do not show that the insane come hither, but that the coming makes them insane. The reasons are evident and full of warning significance. Immigration is an act fraught with tremendous risks, not only to those who undertake it, but to those among whom it is consummated. It is not only a religious but a political truth that the bounds of our habitations are appointed. No man should break over them without the best of reasons and distinct fitness; least of all should the weak and the ignorant, for the simple reason that they most need a molding and restraining environment. When such come hither, they are practically without environment, being too ignorant to perceive and come under that which exists. Concretely stated, such immigrants do not become Americans. Hence that social and political condition which now so obtrudes itself upon public attention,—anarchism, lawlessness, hoodlumism, pauperism, boycottism, labor strikes, and a general violation of personal rights such as the Anglo-Saxon race has not witnessed since Magna Charta. The combined tyranny of Europe during the last half-century does not afford such a spectacle of cruel and unreasonable tyranny, of trampling upon personal freedom, as that witnessed in the United States during the last three or four years. This horrible tyranny is wholly of foreign origin,—the plain and simple fruit of ignorance of American institutions and of the meaning of the word *rights.* If we suffer from this, we have ourselves to thank for it. We invoked ignorance, and it is tormenting us with its proper weapons. The negro problem aside, there is scarcely a great public evil in this nation but has its roots in this indiscriminate immigration. It is the foreign element that poisons politics, blocks the wheels of industry, fills our prisons and hospitals and poor-houses, defies law, perplexes our schemes of education, lowers the grade of public virtue, atheizes the state, confuses labor, supplants the caucus by the saloon, feeds the drink-evil, and turns municipal government into a farce and a shame.

The Passport

It is getting to be felt in many quarters that this process has gone far enough, and that it may be well to exchange our grand idealism for a little common sense and practical statesmanship. The passport seems to be the only available means of restricting immigration so as to exclude that which is undesirable. No scrutiny by a commission in our ports will turn back any considerable number. The restriction must be made before the journey hither begins. For this purpose the consulate could easily be employed. It is not proposed to prohibit foreign immigration; but it is proposed to make it, at least, not so easy a matter as it is at present. To this end it is suggested that laws be enacted requiring every person to show before an American official his fitness to become an American citizen,—laws strong on the negative side, shutting out the grossly degraded and ignorant, the physically degenerate, the criminal; and still stronger on the positive side, requiring some inceptive preparation for entering into American life, and some real intention to fall into the current of the national life and to support its institutions.

We are aware that a government cannot do everything that needs to be done for its people; also that human society, as distinct from government, must work out many of its problems without the aid of law, and that, being an organism, it is fitted to do this. We are also aware that social regeneration must be largely left to science and ethical teaching and religion. Society has laws and forces of its own which work towards the elimination of evil and the creation of good and require no aid from the civil law. But these social forces presuppose a normal constitution of society,— potentially, at least. When society is suffered by law, or by the absence of law, to become abnormally constituted,—heterogeneous, ill-balanced, overweighted with bad elements alien to itself,—then civil law may be invoked to take off the hindrances, and thus make the way clear for society to enforce its own redemptive methods.

Viewpoint 4

"The immigrants who arrive at our shores are for the most part good material out of which to make American citizens."

The Proper Class of Immigrant Should Not Be Restricted

Simon Greenleaf Croswell

One argument used by those supporting restrictions on immigration in the nineteenth century was that the large numbers of immigrants to the United States were overcrowding cities, especially along the eastern seaboard. Simon Greenleaf Croswell counters that contention by arguing in the following viewpoint that the United States, except for its major cities, has a low population density—much lower than the countries in Europe, where many of the immigrants hailed from. Because of America's low population density, the demand for labor exceeds the available supply. Therefore, he asserts, the argument that the United States should restrict immigration due to overcrowding is baseless. Instead, Croswell maintains that the United States should encourage immigration to meet the demand for labor, as most immigrants are hard workers who would make good

Simon Greenleaf Croswell, "Should Immigration Be Restricted?" *North American Review*, April 1897.

American citizens. Croswell was a lawyer and law professor at
Harvard Law School.

D uring recent years there has been a growing interest in devising some plan for checking or limiting the tide of immigration whose waves sweep in upon the United States almost daily
in constantly increasing volume. The subject has been discussed
in legislatures, in political meetings, from pulpits, in reform clubs,
and among individuals on every hand. The reason for the interest which the subject now excites is easily found in the recent
enormous increase of immigration.

Much as the subject has been discussed, however, and many as
have been the arguments which have been brought forward on
one side or the other, there has been a noticeable lack of the one
element which can give certainty to the arguments and force to
the conclusions. Inferences, deductions, conjectures, and a host
of less persuasive probabilities have been brought forward and pa-
raded in each line of battle; but of facts, such facts, I mean, as bear
directly and strongly upon the problems involved, there has been
little use made. The purpose of this article is to set forth clearly
and prominently these facts, to investigate them, and see to what
conclusions they point.

The problem divides itself at the outset into two distinct questions: First, is it for the advantage of the United States that immigration be checked or limited? Second, if so, in what way should
the check or limit be applied?

It will not do to trust to the answers to these questions given by
local interests or party prejudices. If these interests and prejudices
were to be consulted, we should hear in answer to the first question, a loud and emphatic "yes" from the Eastern seaboard, and
from the great centers of population on the east slope of the Alleghanies. In these Eastern cities, where the already crowded me-
chanic and artisan and laborer view in each new arrival a possible
competitor and rival, local feeling would be strongly in favor of a
limitation of the immigration. On the other hand, from the central States in the Mississippi Valley, where the existing population
has not risen to so high a percentage, compared with the sup-

porting powers of the land, and where the demand for unskilled labor which the immigrants are qualified to perform is still in excess of the supply, the answer would not be so distinct and emphatic. There would be good reasons advanced by one party why immigration should be encouraged, rather than checked, while another party would assert that there were already too many immigrants and that some limit must be fixed. Going still further West, where the average percentage of population to the area of the land dwindles in some localities almost to the vanishing point, we should hear from the isolated inhabitants who are wrestling with nature on their scattered farms and ranches, a cry for laborers, as distinct and emphatic, if not uttered by so great numbers, as the opposing cry in the East. . . .

Taking up . . . the industrial question, we may assume that the entrance of the swarms of immigrants into our country represents the introduction of just so much laboring power into the country, and we may also assume as a self-evident proposition that the introduction of laboring power into an undeveloped or partially developed country is advantageous until the point is reached at which all the laborers whom the country can support have been introduced. [Scottish economist and philosopher] Adam Smith says that labor is the wealth of nations. If this is true, the laborer is the direct and only primary means of acquiring wealth. The facts of the history of our country bear out this view. Beginning with the clearing of the forests, the settlement of the villages, the cultivation of farms, proceeding to the establishment of the lumber industries, the cultivation of vast wheat and corn fields, the production of cotton, the working of the coal and oil fields of Pennsylvania, the development of the mining districts of the West, culminating in the varied and extensive manufactures of the Eastern and Central States, the laborer has been the Midas whose touch has turned all things to gold.

There is, however, a limitation to the principle that the introduction of laborers into a partially developed country is advantageous. A point is finally reached which may be called the saturation point of the country; that is, it has as many inhabitants as it can supply with reasonably good food and clothing. This saturation point may be reached many times in the history of a country, for the ratio between the food and clothing products and the population is constantly varying. New modes of cultivation, and the use of machinery, as well as natural causes affecting the fertility of land, which are as yet obscure, render a country at one time capable of supporting a much larger number of inhabitants than at another time. Still, there is a broad and general truth that, time and place and kind of people being considered, some countries are over-populated, and some are under-populated.

We are accustomed to say that some of the countries of Europe are over-populated, and there are among us some who are beginning to say that the United States have reached the same point. This is far from being the case, and a single glance at the comparative average density of population of the principal European nations and of the United States will be sufficient to drive this idea out of any fair minded person's head.

The most thickly settled country of modern Europe is the Netherlands, which had, in the year 1890, the very large average of 359 inhabitants per square mile of territory. Great Britain came next with the almost equally large average of 311 inhabitants per square mile of territory. Germany had 234 and France 187. Taking in for purposes of comparison, though not of much force in the argument, China, we find there an average population of 295 inhabitants per square mile of territory. It is a question of some difficulty to decide in any specific case whether a country has reached the point of over-population. We may admit that Great Britain, with its average of 311 inhabitants per mile, is over-populated, though the conditions of life do not seem to be wholly intolerable, even to the lowest classes there. If Great Britain is over-populated, *a fortiori* are the Netherlands, and we may even go so far as to admit that Germany, with its average of 234 inhabitants per square mile, is over-populated. But when we come to France, with its 187 inhabitants per square mile, we may pause and see what are the conditions of the French people. So far as it is possible to judge of a people in the lump, it would seem that the population of France is not excessive for the area. The land holdings are divided up into very small lots, but are held by a great number of people. Mackenzie, in his history of the nineteenth century, says that nearly two-thirds of the French householders

The New Colossus

In 1886 the French gave the Statue of Liberty to Americans as a token of friendship between the two countries. Officially titled Liberty Enlightening the World, the statue was created by French artist Frédéric-Auguste Bartholdi to symbolize the abstract concepts of liberty and freedom that the United States represented to the world. Years after the dedication of the statue, New York poet Emma Lazarus wrote the following poem, "The New Colossus" (a reference to the Colossus of Rhodes statue of the Greek god Apollo and one of the original Seven Wonders of the World), as part of a fund-raiser for the statue's pedestal. The poem was engraved on a plaque at the base of the statue. Since the Statue of Liberty was one of the first sights of America for millions of immigrants passing by on their way to Ellis Island, the statue came to be seen as a symbol welcoming them to their new home.

Not like the brazen giant of Greek fame,
With conquering limbs astride from land to land,
Here at our sea-washed, sunset gates shall stand
A mighty woman with a torch, whose flame
Is the imprisoned lightning, and her name
Mother of Exiles. From her beacon-hand
Glows world-wide welcome; her mild eyes command
The air-bridged harbor that twin cities frame.

"Keep, ancient lands, your storied pomp!" cries she
With silent lips. "Give me your tired, your poor,
Your huddled masses yearning to breathe free,
The wretched refuse of your teeming shore.
Send these, the homeless, tempest-tost to me,
I lift my lamp beside the golden door!"

Emma Lazarus, "The New Colossus," in John Higham, *Send These to Me: Jews and Other Immigrants in Urban America.* New York: Atheneum, 1975, p. 78.

are landowners, while only one British householder in every four is an owner of land. This condition results partly from the difference in the system of inheritance of land in the two countries, but would be impossible if the country were over-populated. Moreover, there are five millions of people in France whose possessions in land are under six acres each.

Taking, then, the population of France, averaging 187 per square mile, as being at least not above the normal rate of population, what do we find in comparing it with the population of the United States? We find over here vast tracts of country, amounting to nearly one-third by actual measurement, of the whole area of the United States, and including all the States west of the Missouri and Mississippi valleys (except a portion of California), having a population of less than six individuals per square mile. It would seem as if the mere statement of this fact were alone sufficient to disprove any proposition which asserts that the saturation point of population has been reached in the United States. While that immense expanse of country averages only 6 individuals to the square mile, there can be no reason for saying that this country is over-populated. Coming now to the more thickly settled portions of the United States, we find a large area spread out over various parts of the States having a population of between seven and forty-five individuals per square mile. In a very few States, New York, Pennsylvania, Michigan, Ohio, and Indiana, the population of the whole State averages over forty-five and under ninety individuals per square mile, and the same average holds in parts of Massachusetts, Connecticut, Illinois, Kentucky, and isolated spots in the South. In a small territory, made up of parts of Massachusetts, Pennsylvania, and New Jersey, the population averages over ninety per square mile.

The contrast between these averages of population in various portions of the United States, the highest of which is about ninety individuals per mile (and that over very small portions of the area of the United States) and the average densities of the European countries, previously examined, shows how very far the United States still is from complete population. This appears still more clearly when the average population of the United States, taken as a whole, is considered, which is the extraordinarily low figure of twenty individuals per square mile of territory. What a striking contrast! Can the most ardent advocate of the Malthusian doctrine [a doctrine written by Thomas Malthus (1766–1834) stating that population growth will be limited by death from starvation when food resources run out] claim that the United States already has too many inhabitants, or is in danger of having too many in the immediate future? Do we not rather need to encourage immigration, to fling wide open the gates of our country and secure as large an addition to our working force as possible?

There is, however, a limit to immigration which should be invariably applied. The reason why the encouragement of immigration is desirable from an industrial point of view is simply that it furnishes more laborers. Necessarily, therefore, those who are unable or unwilling to work should be excluded. . . .

The immigrants who arrive at our shores are for the most part good material out of which to make American citizens, if they are properly trained. . . . The two conspicuous defects in these immigrants are lack of general education and lack of special training in free political institutions. Applying these conclusions to the questions which were stated at the outset of this article; first, is it for the advantage of the United States that immigration should be checked or limited? second, if so, in what way should the check or limit be applied? the answer would be that no check or limit should be applied to the immigration of *bona fide* laborers, but that a check should be placed upon the exercise of the franchise by immigrants in all States by requiring a residence of five years in this country before they can vote, and by also requiring some moderate educational test.

With these safeguards established we might look without any serious apprehension upon the increase of our population. The founders of our state moulded the outlines of its form in large and noble lines. The skeleton has grown and clothed itself with flesh with almost incredible rapidity in the hundred years of its existence. But it is still young. We should avoid any measures which would stunt or deform its growth and should allow it to develop freely and generously till the full-grown American nation stands forth pre-eminent among the nations of the earth, in size, as well as in character and organization, and man's last experiment in government is clearly seen to be an unequivocal success.

Viewpoint 5

"When . . . a nation reaches a stage where it finds its own birthrate declining, and immigrants with a much larger birthrate flocking into the country, the time has come for very serious consideration as to the means to be taken for self-preservation."

The High Immigrant Birthrate Threatens Native Stock

Alexander Graham Bell

Alexander Graham Bell is best known as the inventor of the telephone. Born in Scotland, he became a U.S. citizen in 1882. In the following viewpoint, Bell discusses the threat posed by immigrants who reproduce at a higher rate than white Americans. He contends that if Americans do not have greater numbers of children, they will be displaced by highly fertile immigrants who will ultimately overwhelm and absorb the American white race. Therefore, in order to protect native Americans from "race suicide," restrictions must be imposed to reduce the number of immigrants entering the United States.

One of the most interesting of the questions of today relates to the powerful influence exerted upon populations by what we

Alexander Graham Bell, "Is Race Suicide Possible?" *Journal of Heredity*, November 1920.

might almost call negative selection. A selection that produces the very opposite of that expected.

For example, no inheritable peculiarity associated with lack of offspring can be made to grow and flourish in a community. In spite of all efforts it will languish, and promote the growth of its very opposite. History is full of illustrations.

Celibacy

After the fall of the Roman Empire there was a great religious revival among the nations. The Middle Ages saw Europe filled with monasteries and nunneries, where enormous numbers of people took vows of celibacy, and renounced all home and family ties. Even outside of the religious houses the *celibate life* was everywhere held up as the ideal one to be followed by the best and purest elements of the population.

Instead of helping the church this produced the very opposite effect, and actually paved the way for the Reformation! Large masses of the people who were most attached to the Church led celibate lives, and left no descendants, whereas the independently minded who were not so devoted to the Church were not limited in their reproduction.

As to the more general effects it may be safely said that the worship of celibacy during several hundreds of years in the past has not tended to the improvement of humanity but the very reverse; for, where the best and noblest led celibate lives, they left no descendants behind them to inherit their virtues, whereas the worst elements of the population continued to multiply without restriction.

It is now felt that the interests of the race demand that the best should marry and have large families; and that any restrictions upon reproduction should apply to the worst rather than to the best.

It is of course useless to expect that the worst would take vows of celibacy or keep them; and the realization of this has led to all sorts of impracticable schemes to prevent or restrict their reproduction by compulsory means.

The great trouble about all these schemes, apart from their impracticability, is that they aim simply to prevent degeneration. They aim to prevent the race from moving backwards, but do not help it to move forwards. The only hope of producing higher and better types of men and women lies in the multiplication of the better elements of the population.

There is one very promising feature about the present situation, and that is that the best are readily attracted by high ideals. Give them a new ideal, and many will follow it, especially if they believe that duty points in the same direction. Convince them that the interests of the race demand that the best should increase and multiply; convince them that it is therefore their duty to marry, rather than lead celibate lives. Depose "celibacy" from the high and commanding position she has occupied for so many hundred years, and put "marriage" there instead as the ideal to be held up before the best and noblest of the race. Marriage, with marriage vows as sacred as the former vows of celibacy. Nature demands this in the interests of the race. For the extreme helplessness of the human infant necessitates parental care for very prolonged periods of time—in fact at least from infancy to the beginning of adult life—and this involves the permanency of the marital tie on the part of the parents, especially where a number of children are produced.

Race Suicide

At the present time considerable alarm has been expressed at the apparently growing disinclination of American women to bear children, and a cry has been raised against what people call "Race Suicide." Whatever the cause—it is undoubtedly the fact that in America the children of foreign-born parents are increasing at a much greater rate than the children of native-born parents—and the position is sufficiently grave for serious consideration.

The desire to avoid maternity is a characteristic associated with lack of offspring, and cannot therefore go on increasing indefinitely in a community. Its natural tendency is to die out through lack of offspring to inherit it, leaving the more fertile part of the community alone to propagate the race.

Reflection therefore leads to the somewhat startling conclusion that even wholesale abstention from children, so far from lessening the fertility of the community as a whole will eventually increase it instead. Actual race suicide will not result from such a cause alone, so long as the race is left to itself to work out its own destiny.

Just consider the case of a race of people in which the women show a disinclination for motherhood, surrounded by prolific immigrant races ready to take its place, then of course there would be serious danger of the native race being displaced by the immigrants. The immigrants might absorb the native race instead of the native race absorbing the immigrants; but such a result would be due to the presence of the competing races and not due directly to the operation of natural causes within the race itself.

The Destiny of an Island Race

In order to appreciate this, imagine our native race to be placed upon an island protected by suitable immigration laws from competition with other races. Then it becomes obvious that the sentiment in favor of avoiding the production of offspring must necessarily diminish in process of time, on account of the lack of offspring to inherit it; and that the opposite sentiment of a desire to have children will grow, and ultimately become predominant, because each succeeding generation will be composed exclusively of the descendants of the people who had children. If the desire for offspring is an inheritable characteristic, *and it certainly is*, then of course the next generation will inherit it from their parents to a certain extent; whereas there will be no descendants at all to inherit the characteristics of those who abstained from offspring.

We have placed the people upon an island, and protected them from interference from other races, so as to leave them to themselves to carry on their lives in their own way, as they desire.

Some of these people love little children, and desire to have children of their own. Others look upon children as nuisances, perhaps necessary evils for the continuance of the race—but why should they be bothered with them when they don't want them? Let others have them if they want them, but leave *them* alone. Well—let them have their desires.

Let those who desire children have them, and those who don't, have none, and see how it will all work out.

Now does it not become at once evident that so long as any of the people desire offspring and have them, complete race suicide is impossible? Some offspring will be produced and a second generation will appear.

Suppose for example the boom against maternity reaches such proportions that 99 per cent of the population decide to have no children—and surely this is an extreme case—will the race die out? No—not immediately at all events. There will be another generation composed exclusively of the descendants of the one per cent who desire to have children. The whole of the next generation will be composed of their children; and there will be no descendants at all of the other ninety-nine per cent.

This is the critical time for our islanders. Only one per cent of the population have had children, and of course the numbers in the next generation will be so seriously reduced that immigration from outside would speedily swamp them—but we have agreed to protect them from this competition with other races, and leave them alone to work out their destiny to the bitter end.

Well, let us revisit the island after the original population has passed away. We find the population now only a fraction of what it was before; and the question naturally arises: will the population continue to diminish at each successive generation until actual race suicide results?

It is not to be supposed that the sentiment against maternity will disappear in one generation. The second generation will therefore undoubtedly continue to be divided upon the question of maternity; some wishing to have children, others not; but the *proportion* desiring children will necessarily be greater, on account of heredity, than in the original population; for the whole of this second generation are descended from the one per cent who desired offspring whereas the ninety-nine per cent who did not desire them left no descendants.

There seems to be no escape from the conclusion that in this second generation more than one per cent of the people will desire children, and less than ninety-nine per cent will abstain from their production. Therefore the proportion of the second generation who will have children will be greater than in the first, and the proportion opposed to maternity will be less.

Thus in each succeeding generation the proportion who desire children and have them will increase, and the proportion avoiding maternity diminish, with the net result that each succeeding generation will be more fertile than the last. The desire to avoid maternity will die out to a great extent on account of the lack of offspring to inherit it. *The spirit of race suicide will itself commit suicide, and leave a more fertile race than before.*

The only thing that could prevent such a result would be: the admission of immigrants during the period of declining birthrate.

This indeed is the critical period in the history not only of our hypothetical islanders, but of every nation similarly situated. When therefore a nation reaches a stage where it finds its own birthrate declining, and immigrants with a much larger birthrate flocking into the country, the time has come for very serious consideration as to the means to be taken for self-preservation.

The United States is today in this critical position. The birthrate of America is declining; the spirit of avoiding maternity is on the increase; and the immigrant races are increasing at a much greater rate than our own. The only hope for a truly American race lies in the restriction of immigration.

Viewpoint 6

*"Our apprehension of harm to American ideals
from race mixture is nothing but prejudice."*

The New Immigrants Do Not Threaten America's Racial Stock

Percy Stickney Grant

In the following viewpoint, Percy Stickney Grant states that he
does not believe the new wave of immigrants arriving at the turn
of the century are detrimental to American society. He argues
that fears about the new immigrants "weakening" America's
racial stock are nothing more than irrational prejudice. Furthermore, science supports the idea that mixing races through interracial marriage results in a stronger people. In addition, immigrants quickly adapt to American ideals. Grant also asserts that
nurture plays a more important role in developing a person's
character than nature. Grant was an author and a minister of an
Episcopal church in New York City. He wrote several works on
social issues, including *Fair Play and the Workers*, *Socialism and
Christianity*, and *Religion on Main Street*.

Percy Stickney Grant, *North American Review*, April 1912.

The most impressive sight to be seen in America is the stream of immigrants coming off ship at Ellis Island. No waterfall or mountain holds such awesome mystery; no river or harbor, embracing the navies of the world, expresses such power; no city so puts wings to the imagination; no work of art calls with such epic beauty. But there are spectators who behold in the procession from overseas an invading army comparable to the Gothic hordes that overran Rome, who lament this meeting of Europe and America as the first act in our National Tragedy.

Undoubtedly we have a situation unknown to any other nation, past or present. In 1910 the total population of the United States was 91,972,266; of these 13,343,583 were foreign-born whites; 10,239,579 were negroes, Indians, and Asiatics. Between 1900–1910, 9,555,673 immigrants came in from over fifty races. Of the native whites forty-seven per cent. are the children of foreign-born parents. Of our entire population 43,972,185 were born of native white parents—that is, only forty per cent.

A recent writer in *The North American Review*, Prescott F. Hall, secretary of the League for Limiting Immigration and author of a volume on immigration, stated in the January number the case against the future of American ideals under the influence of race mixture. He began by quoting [French diplomat and writer Joseph Arthur] Gobineau: "America is likely to be not the cradle of a new, but the grave of an old race." Mr. Hall sought to sustain this prophecy.

I belong to no immigration league, "limiting" or "liberal"; I have had no admixture of blood in my own family, outside the original area of Massachusetts, for two hundred years, but I wish to suggest considerations that may calm the fears of Mr. Hall and his friends. . . .

Fears Caused by Prejudice

Broadly speaking, our apprehension of harm to American ideals from race mixture is nothing but prejudice. Much of our dread of a deterioration of the American stock by immigration is a survival of ancient jealousy and alarm which once characterized the contact of all "natives" everywhere with all "foreigners." The sight of a foreigner meant ordinarily a raid or a war. This real dread, as it was of old, lingers in our subconsciousness. The destruction of the trait will yield only to intelligence, sympathy, and civilization.

Another element in our fear is the fetish of Teutonic superiority and the dogma of Latin degeneracy. Races that have produced in our lifetime a [Camillo Benso di] Cavour, a [Giuseppe] Mazzini [both Italian independence leaders], a Louis Pasteur [French inventor of the process of pasteurization], that have fought and defeated ecclesiastic and feudal enemies in their own households, have much to teach us.

In the Conference on Immigration held in New York a few years ago, there were delegates scarcely able to speak the English language who orated against later arrivals in this country than themselves and predicted our downfall if they were admitted. In short, every race considers itself superior; its diatribes against other races are sheer vanity. We Americans, in conceit of superiority, are in the same class as the Chinese. William Elliot Griffis, a writer on Asiatic people, recently declared that

> after an adult lifetime of study of the peoples of the Far East,
> I find few or no novelties in their history or evolution as com-
> pared with that of our own rise from savagery to civilization;
> nor is their human nature by a hair's-breadth different from
> our own. What we need now to have cast in the world's
> melting-pot is the colossal conceit common to the white and
> the yellow man with more scientific comparative history.

At any rate, our free government is a standing invitation to the oppressed of other countries, and our undeveloped wealth makes a constant appeal for strong arms and hard workers. What can we do, then? We cannot shut out "foreigners" and still be true either to our own ideals or to our practical requirements. Nor can we pick and choose. There is no accepted standard of excellence except health and "literacy." Moreover, there are not enough of one foreign stock, were we to select one as the best, to do the work in the United States waiting to be done. . . .

Scientific Attitude Toward Heredity

The scientific attitude toward heredity is to-day different from a generation ago. [Charles] Darwin's theory of slowly acquired char-

acteristics and of the transmission by heredity of acquired characteristics was attacked by August Weismann, whose germ-plasm
theory of heredity seriously weakened Darwin's hypothesis. Then
came the botanist, [Hugo] De Vries, with his theory of spasmodic
progress, amounting to "spasmodic appearance of species at a
given time under the influence of certain special conditions."

Francis Galton brought forward the theory of mathematical inheritance, which, modified by [Karl] Pearson, amounts to this:
That of all the heritage which an individual possesses one-half on
the average comes from his parents, one-fourth from his grandparents, and so on. Meanwhile the studies of Gregor Mendel, Ab-
bot of Brünn, neglected for thirty-five years after their publication
in 1865, came to light, with a specific body of botanical experi-
ments leading to certain general principles of heredity. The essential part of Mendel's discoveries is the principle of the segregation
of characters in the fusion of the reproductive cells or gametes,
with its natural corollary, the purity of the gametes. Mendel did
not believe in blends, but in the unit character of heredity.

Two theories of heredity are now current:

> 1. Children show a tendency to revert to a type intermediate
> between the types of the two parents, or in cases of changes
> of types to another type, dependent upon the mid-parental
> type. In other words, the characteristics of the parents are
> blended in the children.

> 2. Either the father's or the mother's type, or the type of a
> more remote ancestor, is reproduced, and certain parental
> traits may be dominant over others—*i.e.*, one particular trait,
> either father's or mother's, to appear with greater frequency
> in the children than the corresponding but different trait of
> the other parent. (*Change in Bodily Form of Descendants of
> Immigrants*, by Franz Boas.)

An inquiry into the values of a cephalic index (that is, the ratio
of the width of the head to the length) has shown clearly that the
type of heredity in intermarriages in the same race is that of alternating heredity. Children do not form a blend between their
parents, but revert either to one type or the other.

Mendel's law attaches so much value to "dominant" and so much danger to "recessive" units that under his theory, it would be natural to try to divide races into the old categories of sheep and goats. But even under the operation of his law a mixed race has advantages over a pure race. [Charles B. Davenport writes in the *Annals of American Academy:*]

> The clear lesson of Mendelian studies to human society is this: That when two parents with the same defect marry—and there is none of us without some defect—*all* of the progeny must have the same defect, and there is no remedy for the defect by education, but only, at the most in a few cases, by a surgical operation. The presence of a character in one parent will dominate over its absence in the other parent; . . . the advanced position masters the retarded or absent condition.

[He adds:] *"The mating of dissimilars favors a combination in the offspring of the strongest characteristics of both parents and fits them the better for human society."* A strong argument for miscegeneration.

Environment More Important than Heredity

Environment to-day is considered a most important factor in heredity by students outside the ranks of pure biologists. Take such a fact as this, that the intellectual classes among the Magyars, the Uralo-Altaic peoples, the Slavs or German races, furnish us with identical measurements of trunk, extremities, etc., whereas individuals of the same race differ considerably when once distinctly separated by their occupations. Another fact in the same direction is that the measurements of Austrian Jews correspond entirely with those that Gould mentioned in the case of cultivated persons in the United States. The Austrian Jews are not engaged in mercantile work, but almost exclusively are money-lenders, small shop-keepers, lawyers, and doctors [according to Jean Finot in his book *Race Prejudice*].

We all agree with Professor Ripley that

> the first impression from comparison of our original Anglo-Saxon ancestry in America with the motley crowd now pouring in upon us is not cheering. It seems a hopeless task to cope

with them, to assimilate them with our present native-born population.

But listen further:

> Yet there are distinctly encouraging features about it all. These people, in the main, have excellent physical qualities, in spite of unfavorable environment and political oppression for generations. No finer physical type than the peasantry of Austro-Hungary are to be found in Europe. The Italians, with an out-of-door life and proper food, are not weaklings. Nor is even the stunted and sedentary Jew—the third greatest in our present immigrant hordes—an unfavorable vital specimen. Their careful religious regulations have produced in them a longevity even under most unfavorable conditions. Even to-day, under normal conditions, a rough process of selection is at work to bring the better types to our shores. We receive, in the main, the best, the most progressive and alert of the peasantry that the lower classes which these lands recently tapped, are able to offer. This is a feature of no mean importance. Barring artificial selection by steamship companies and police, we need not complain in the main of the physique of new arrivals.

"The great problem for us in dealing with these immigrants is not that of their nature, but that of their nurture," [writes Ripley].
[E.A. Ross writes in the *Annals American of Academy:*]

> We Americans who have so often seen the children of under-fed, stunted, scrub immigrants match the native American in brain and brawn ought to realize how much the superior effectiveness of the matter is due to social conditions. The cause of race superiority is a physiological trait—namely, climatic adaptability.

The races coming to America show power of adaptation. But as this power of adaptation must be slow, we must be patient. It was slow among the best of the early colonists. [Jenks and Lauck write in *The Immigration Problem*], *"The adaptability of the various races coming together on our shores seem, if these indications be borne out by further study, to be much greater than had been expected."*
[E.A. Ross agrees:]

> *Not merely do the children of immigrants in many instances show greater height and weight than the same races in their mother country, but in some instances even the head form, which has always been considered one of the most stable and permanent characteristics of races, undergoes very great changes.*

> But the important fact to be kept in mind is that whatever the cause may be, and whether the change in type is for the better or worse, the *influence of the new environment is very marked indeed, and we may therefore expect that the degree and ease of assimilation has probably been somewhat greater than has been heretofore assumed. . . .*

Professor Earl Finch presents "some facts tending to prove that race blending, especially in the rare instances when it occurs under favorable circumstances, produces a type superior in fertility, vitality, and cultural worth to one or both of the parent stocks."

This view was maintained, on the whole, in the preliminary discussion of the last Congress of Races, the manifest exceptions to the statement being explicable mainly by the unsatisfactory social conditions of the half-breeds—in other words, *the problems of miscegenation are sociological rather than physiological.*

All Races Equal in Mental Ability

Professor Franz Boas, of Columbia University, in a recent volume, *The Mind of Primitive Man*, defends the proposition that there is a substantial equality in the native mental ability of all races of mankind; that the inferiority of races is not due to any lack of native ability, but to the accidents which have prevented them from sharing in the fruits of the discoveries made by individual geniuses. He finds that "the characteristics of the osseous, muscular, visceral, and circulatory system have practically no direct relation to the mental ability of men"; and that the size of the brain is so nearly alike in all races that no inferences can be drawn from the facts collected. "It is not impossible that the smaller brains of males of other races should do the same work as is done by the larger brain of the white race." He contends that "the civilizations of ancient Peru and Central America may well be compared with the ancient civilizations of the Old World." *In view of his investigations, the author does not fear the effects of the intermingling of races in America.*

Says Professor Ripley: "Going back far enough, it is clear that all the peoples of Europe are a hodge-podge of different stocks." Going back as far as we please to the Aryans, we find, some scholars claim, a mixed race. "*Le terme d'Aryen est de pure convention* [A pure Aryan race does not exist,]" [quotes Chamberlain]. In addition to this sort of general evidence, there is material of a more definite kind. Distinguished men have an ancestry of a mongrel sort.

> [French novelist] Alexandre Dumas (West-Indian negro blood); [American patriot and contributor to the Constitution] Alexander Hamilton (French and English); Du Maurier and St.-Gaudens, Dante Gabriel Rosetti [English painter with Italian parents] stand for still greater strains of bonds of nationality. [Greek writer] Lafcadio Hearn (Greek and Irish). These few examples show that intermixture is, at all events, not destructive in its effect.

Take, too, such a case as [English poet] Robert Browning, who was rather proud of the fact that he was the product of four strains of European blood.

No Pure Races Exist

Drs. von Luschan and Haddon agree that there are practically no pure races still existing, and that a discussion of races is mainly of academic interest. The former goes so far as to state that the old Indo-European, the African, and the Asiatic all branched off from the same primitive stock, perhaps hundreds of years ago, but all three forming a complete unit, intermarrying in all directions without the slightest decrease of fertility.

Even American families have been much beholden to "foreign" blood. Wendell Phillips and Phillips Brooks would be regarded by most people as fine products of the Anglo-Saxon stock. Both had Du Maurier's "drop of Hebrew blood." Professor Sombart credits the Jews with furnishing one frontiersman to every four in the era of American beginnings.

The unfavorable mixture of South-American races with Indians and negroes cited by Prescott F. Hall is not a fair parallel with the mixture of European races. It leaves out of account the European and American *milieu*—education, marriage, the home, and high political institutions.

There seems some distinct limits put by nature upon the mixture of certain races, just as there is to the blending of blood which has become badly vitiated. Nature puts a final veto upon propagation in such directions. There would seem to be, then, a friendly hand held out by nature itself to prevent disastrous results in race admixture.

Another interesting side to this question, however, is seen particularly in the Orient, where the Chinese have mixed with many peoples, as, for instance, the Hawaiians, Filipinos, and Malays. These Mestizos are recognized in the Orient as particularly clever, the reason often assigned being that the Chinese protect and educate their children, no matter what the other blood may be, whereas the Eurasian (white and Asiatic mixed) is crippled by the lack of support and education—that is, practical desertion by the white father. . . .

The Roman Empire did not fall on account of racial degeneracy, due to the infiltration of Huns, Goths, and Vandals, but on account of the weakness of its political and industrial institutions, and the enervation of the people in the hands of the patrician class. The Roman land laws and Roman slaves, as well as the Roman system of government, which had no method of true amalgamation, but was a loose sort of confederacy, are responsible for the breakup of the Roman Empire.

Immigrants Quickly Adapt to American Ideals

The rapidity with which the democratic ideas are taken on by immigrants under the influence of our institutions is remarkable. I have personally had experiences with French-Canadians, Portuguese, Hebrews, and Italians. These races have certainly taken advantage of their opportunities among us in a fashion to promise well for their final effect upon this country. The French-Canadian has become a sufficiently good American to have given up his earlier programme of turning New England into a new France—that is, into a Catholic province or of returning to the Province of Quebec. He is seeing something better than a racial or religious ideal in the freedom of American citizenship; and on one or two occasions, when he had political power in two municipalities, he refrained from exercising it to the detriment of the public-school system. He has added a gracious manner and a new feeling for beauty to New England traits.

The Portuguese have taken up neglected or abandoned New England agricultural land and have turned it to productive and valuable use. Both the French-Canadian and the Portuguese have come to us by way of the New England textile mills.

The actual physical machinery of civilization—cotton-mills, woolen-mills, iron-mills, etc.—lock up a great deal of human energy physical and mental, just as one hundred years ago the farms did, from which later sprang most of the members of our dominant industrial class. A better organization of society, by which machinery would do still more and afford a freer play for mental and physical energy and organization, would find a response from classes that are now looked upon as not contributing to our American culture; would unlock the high potentialities in the laboring classes, now unguessed and unexpended.

The intellectual problems and the advanced thinking of the Hebrew, his fondness for study, and his freedom on the whole from wasteful forms of dissipation, sport, and mental stagnation, constitute him a more fortunate acquisition for this country than are thousands of the descendants of Colonial settlers. In short, we must reconstruct our idea of democracy—of American democracy. This done, we must construct a new picture of citizenship. If we do these things we shall welcome the rugged strength of the peasant or the subtle thought of the man of the Ghetto in our reconsidered American ideals. After all, what are these American ideals we boast so much about? Shall we say public schools, the ballot, freedom? The American stock use private schools when they can afford them; they too often leave town on Election Day; as for freedom, competent observers believe it is disappearing. The conservators and believers in American ideals seem to be our immigrants. To the Russian Jew, Abraham Lincoln is a god. If American ideals are such as pay honor to the intellectual and to the spiritual or foster human brotherhood or love culture and promote liberty, then they are safe with our new citizens who are eager for these things.

Not only do these races bring with them most desirable qualities, but they themselves are subjected to new environment and strongly influential conditions. Just here arise duties for the present masters of America. Ought they not to create an industrial, social, and educational environment of the most uplifting sort for our foreign-born citizens?

Immigrant Adaptation

If working-people are obliged to live in unhealthful tenements situated in slums or marsh land, if the saloon is allowed to be their only social center, if they are fought by the rich in every effort to improve their condition, we may expect any misfortune to happen to them and also any fate to befall the State.

What improved *milieu* can do to improve the physique is easily seen on all sides. The increase in the height and weight of Americans in the last few decades is conspicuous. Even the size of American girls and boys has increased, and this increase in size is commonly attributed to the more comfortable conditions of life, to better food, and especially to the popularity of all forms of athletics, and the extension, as in the last twenty-five or thirty years, of the out-of-door and country life. If these factors have made so marked and visible a change in the physique of the children of native-born Americans, why may not the same conditions also contribute an improvement to the more recent immigrant stock?

Our question, then, as to the effect of race mixture is not the rather supercilious one: What are we admitting into America that may possibly injure American ideals? but, What are the old American races doing to perpetuate these ideals? And is not our future as a race, largely by our own fault, in the hands of the peasant races of Europe?

After all, for those who pin their faith to the Baltic and northern European races, there is reason for hope to be found even in current immigration. From 1899 to 1910, the Hebrew, southern Italian, Polish, and Slovak period, of the nine millions who landed in the United States, while there were 377,527 Slovaks and 318,151 Magyars, there were 408,614 English, 586,306 Scandinavians, and 754,375 Germans, and even 136,842 Scotch, 151,774 Finnish, 439,724 Irish, and 20,752 Welsh. Two millions and a half from northern Europe—over twenty-six percent. One million seventy-four thousand are Hebrews, mostly from Russia; and the Russian Jews, according to a most distinguished German Jew, are intellectually the ablest Hebrews in America. If, on the other hand, nearly two millions of the immigrants of the last decade have been southern Italians, let us show them gratitude for their invaluable manual labor, for their willingness, their patience, their power for fast work, and their love of America. Their small stature does not argue their degeneracy. The Romans were small compared to the Goths—small, but well formed and strong. The Japanese are also small.

Indifference, prejudice, illiteracy, segregation of recent immigrants by parochial schools, by a native colonial press, bad physical and social environment, and the low American ideals of citizenship held by those the immigrant sees or hears most about, obstruct race assimilation; but all these can be changed. Yes, it is the keeping up of difference and class isolation that destroys and deteriorates. Fusion is a law of progress.

Optimistic Thought on Race Mixture

Lastly, let us observe that the men who hold a brief for the "foreigner" are largely men of science from the faculties of our American colleges. Ripley of Harvard, Giddings and Boas of Columbia, and Mayo-Smith (now dead), Jenks of Cornell, Patten and Kelsey of the University of Pennsylvania. The best thought and the best teaching of the country on race mixture is optimistic and constructive. Is it not also significant that an alienist like Dr. Dana is not dismayed by the immigrant, but is hopeful of his contribution? All these are scientific witnesses and are on the spot.

Every act of religious or civil tyranny, every economic wrong done to races in all the world, becomes the burden of the nation to which the oppressed flee for relief and opportunity. And the beauty of democracy is that it is a method by which these needs may freely express themselves and bring about what the oppressed have prayed for and have been denied. Let us be careful not to put America into the class of the oppressors. Let us rise to an eminence higher than that occupied by Washington or Lincoln, to a new Americanism which is not afraid of the blending in the western world of races seeking freedom. Our present problem is the greatest in our history. Not colonial independence, not Federal unity, but racial amalgamation is the heroic problem of the present, with all it implies in purification and revision of old social, religious, and political ideals, with all it demands in new sympathy outside of blood and race, and in a willingness to forgo old-time privileges.

The familiar words of Israel Zangwill will bear repeating—that modern prophet from the race that gave to the world Jesus—when, from a steamer in New York Harbor, he broods over America:

> There she lies, the great Melting Pot. Listen! Can't you hear the roaring and the bubbling? There gapes her mouth—the harbor where a thousand mammoth feeders come from the ends of the world to pour in their human freight. Ah, what a stirring and a seething! Celt and Latin, Slav and Teuton, Greek and Syrian—black and yellow. Yes, East and West, and North and South, the palm and the pine, the pole and the equator, the crescent and the cross—how the great Alchemist melts and fuses them with his purging flame! Here shall they all unite to build the Republic of Man and the Kingdom of God. Ah, what is the glory of Rome and Jerusalem where all nations and races come to worship and look back, compared with the glory of America, where all races come to labor and look forward.

If America has done anything for an American, it ought to have made him helpful and hopeful toward mankind, especially the poor and oppressed; but science to-day comes to the assistance of democracy and finds the lyric cry of brotherhood in the laws of nature:

> Open thy gates, O thou favored of Heaven,
> Open thy gates to the homeless and poor.
> So shalt thou garner the gifts of the ages—
> From the Northlands their vigor,
> The Southlands their grace,
> In a mystical blending of souls that presages
> The birth of earth's rarest, undreamable race.

Viewpoint 7

"[The continuous immigration of the nineteenth and early twentieth centuries] infused the nation with a commitment to far horizons and new frontiers, and thereby kept the pioneer spirit of American life . . . always alive and strong."

The Great Wave Benefited the United States

John F. Kennedy

John F. Kennedy was the thirty-fifth president (1961–1963) of the United States. In the following viewpoint, Kennedy maintains that, since all Americans are immigrants or the descendants of immigrants, it is difficult to discuss a particular "immigrant contribution" to America. However, he adds, each wave of immigration has left its own stamp on the United States and American life, thus contributing to the building of America. Immigrants—well known and anonymous alike—from all countries have made important contributions to science, industry, politics, and the arts. But perhaps the most pervasive influence of immigrants, Kennedy asserts, has been their effect on everyday American life: on religion, vocabulary, and food, for example. In addition, Kennedy contends that the popular image of

John F. Kennedy, *A Nation of Immigrants*. New York: Harper & Row, 1964. Copyright © 1964 by Anti-Defamation League of B'nai B'rith. Reproduced by permission.

the "melting pot" contributes to social equality. At the core of the philosophy that all Americans are created equal is the belief that anyone can better themselves and move up the social and economic ladder, and in the process, build a better nation.

Oscar Handlin has said, "Once I thought to write a history of the immigrants in America. Then I discovered that the immigrants *were* American history." In the same sense, we cannot really speak of a particular "immigrant contribution" to America because all Americans have been immigrants or the descendants of immigrants; even the Indians migrated to the American continent. We can only speak of people whose roots in America are older or newer. Yet each wave of immigration left its own imprint on American society; each made its distinctive "contribution" to the building of the nation and the evolution of American life. Indeed, if, as some of the older immigrants like to do, we were to restrict the definition of immigrants to the 42 million people who came to the United States *after* the Declaration of Independence, we would have to conclude that our history and our society would have been vastly different if they all had stayed at home.

Immigrants Strengthen the Fabric of Liberty

People migrated to the United States for a variety of reasons. But nearly all shared two great hopes: the hope for personal freedom and the hope for economic opportunity. In consequence, the impact of immigration has been broadly to confirm the impulses in American life demanding more political liberty and more economic growth.

So, of the fifty-six signers of the Declaration of Independence, eighteen were of non-English stock and eight were first-generation immigrants. Two immigrants—the West Indian Alexander Hamilton, who was Washington's Secretary of the Treasury, and the Swiss Albert Gallatin, who held the same office under Jefferson—established the financial policies of the young republic. A German farmer wrote home from Missouri in 1834,

If you wish to see our whole family living in . . . a country

> where freedom of speech obtains, where no spies are eaves-
> dropping, where no simpletons criticize your every word and
> seek to detect therein a venom that might endanger the life of
> the state, the church and the home, in short, if you wish to be
> really happy and independent, then come here.

Every ethnic minority, in seeking its own freedom, helped strengthen the fabric of liberty in American life.

The Contributions of Immigrants

Similarly, every aspect of the American economy has profited from the contributions of immigrants. We all know, of course, about the spectacular immigrant successes: the men who came from foreign lands, sought their fortunes in the United States and made striking contributions, industrial and scientific, not only to their chosen country but to the entire world. In 1953 the President's Commission on Immigration and Naturalization mentioned the following:

Industrialists: Andrew Carnegie (Scot), in the steel industry; John Jacob Astor (German), in the fur trade; Michael Cudahy (Irish), of the meat-packing industry; the Du Ponts (French), of the munitions and chemical industry; Charles L. Fleischmann (Hungarian), of the yeast business; David Sarnoff (Russian), of the radio industry; and William S. Knudsen (Danish), of the automobile industry.

Scientists and inventors: Among those whose genius has benefited the United States are Albert Einstein (German), in physics; Michael Pupin (Serbian), in electricity; Enrico Fermi (Italian), in atomic research; John Ericsson (Swedish), who invented the iron-clad ship and the screw propeller; Giuseppe Bellanca (Italian) and Igor Sikorsky (Russian), who made outstanding contributions to airplane development; John A. Udden (Swedish), who was responsible for opening the Texas oil fields; Lucas P. Kyrides (Greek), industrial chemistry; David Thomas (Welsh), who invented the hot blast furnace; Alexander Graham Bell (Scot), who invented the telephone; Conrad Hubert (Russian), who invented the flashlight; and Ottmar Mergenthaler (German), who invented the linotype machine.

But the anonymous immigrant played his indispensable role too. Between 1880 and 1920 America became the industrial and agricultural giant of the world as well as the world's leading creditor nation. This could not have been done without the hard labor, the technical skills and the entrepreneurial ability of the 23.5 million people who came to America in this period.

Significant as the immigrant role was in politics and in the economy, the immigrant contribution to the professions and the arts was perhaps even greater. Charles O. Paullin's analysis of the *Dictionary of American Biography* shows that, of the eighteenth- and nineteenth-century figures, 20 percent of the businessmen, 20 percent of the scholars and scientists, 23 percent of the painters, 24 percent of the engineers, 28 percent of the architects, 29 percent of the clergymen, 46 percent of the musicians and 61 percent of the actors were of foreign birth—a remarkable measure of the impact of immigration on American culture. And not only have many American writers and artists themselves been immigrants or the children of immigrants, but immigration has provided American literature with one of its major themes.

Perhaps the most pervasive influence of immigration is to be found in the innumerable details of life and the customs and habits brought by millions of people who never became famous. This impact was felt from the bottom up, and these contributions to American institutions may be the ones which most intimately affect the lives of all Americans.

In the area of religion, all the major American faiths were brought to this country from abroad. The multiplicity of sects established the American tradition of religious pluralism and assured to all the freedom of worship and separation of church and state pledged in the Bill of Rights.

So, too, in the very way we speak, immigration has altered American life. In greatly enriching the American vocabulary, it has been a major force in establishing "the American language," which, as [American journalist and essayist] H.L. Mencken demonstrated, had diverged materially from the mother tongue as spoken in Britain. Even the American dinner table has felt the impact. One writer has suggested that "typical American menus" might include some of the following dishes: "Irish stew, chop suey, goulash, chile con carne, ravioli, knackwurst mit sauerkraut, Yorkshire pudding, Welsh rarebit, borsch, gefilte fish, Spanish omelet, caviar, mayonnaise, antipasto, baumkuchen, English muffins, Gruyère cheese, Danish pastry, Canadian bacon, hot tamales, wiener schnitzel, petits fours, spumone, bouillabaisse, maté, scones, Turkish coffee, minestrone, filet mignon."

Immigration plainly was not always a happy experience. It was hard on the newcomers, and hard as well on the communities to which they came. When poor, ill-educated and frightened people disembarked in a strange land, they often fell prey to native racketeers, unscrupulous businessmen and cynical politicians. Boss Tweed [a corrupt New York City political "boss" of the nineteenth century] said, characteristically, in defense of his own depredations in New York in the 1870's, "This population is too hopelessly split into races and factions to govern it under universal suffrage, except by bribery of patronage, or corruption."

The Melting Pot

But the very problems of adjustment and assimilation presented a challenge to the American idea—a challenge which subjected that idea to stern testing and eventually brought out the best qualities in American society. Thus the public school became a powerful means of preparing the newcomers for American life. The ideal of the "melting pot" symbolized the process of blending many strains into a single nationality, and we have come to realize in modern times that the "melting pot" need not mean the end of particular ethnic identities or traditions. Only in the case of the Negro has the melting pot failed to bring a minority into the full stream of American life. Today we are belatedly, but resolutely, engaged in ending this condition of national exclusion and shame and abolishing forever the concept of second-class citizenship in the United States.

Sociologists call the process of the melting pot "social mobility." One of America's characteristics has always been the lack of a rigid class structure. It has traditionally been possible for people to move up the social and economic scale. Even if one did not succeed in moving up oneself, there was always the hope that one's children would. Immigration is by definition a gesture of faith in social mobility. It is the expression in action of a positive belief in the possibility of a better life. It has thus contributed greatly to developing the spirit of personal betterment in American society and to strengthening the national confidence in change and the future. Such confidence, when widely shared, sets the national tone. The opportunities that America offered made the dream real, at least for a good many; but the dream itself was in large part the product of millions of plain people beginning a new life in the conviction that life could indeed be better, and each new wave of immigration rekindled the dream.

This is the spirit which so impressed [French writer and sociologist] Alexis de Tocqueville, and which he called the spirit of equality. Equality in America has never meant literal equality of condition or capacity; there will always be inequalities in character and ability in any society. Equality has meant rather that, in the words of the Declaration of Independence, "all men are created equal . . . [and] are endowed by their Creator with certain unalienable rights"; it has meant that in a democratic society there should be no inequalities in opportunities or in freedoms. The American philosophy of equality has released the energy of the people, built the economy, subdued the continent, shaped and reshaped the structure of government and animated the American attitude toward the world outside.

The *continuous* immigration of the nineteenth and early twentieth centuries was thus central to the whole American faith. It gave every old American a standard by which to judge how far he had come and every new American a realization of how far he might go. It reminded every American, old and new, that change is the essence of life, and that American society is a process, not a conclusion. The abundant resources of this land provided the foundation for a great nation. But only people could make the opportunity a reality. Immigration provided the human resources. More than that, it infused the nation with a commitment to far horizons and new frontiers, and thereby kept the pioneer spirit of American life, the spirit of equality and of hope, always alive and strong. "We are the heirs of all time," wrote Herman Melville, "and with all nations we divide our inheritance."

Viewpoint 8

"The most tragic result of the manufacturers' preference for immigrant labor was a half-century postponement of opportunity for most of the freed slaves to seek higher-paying jobs."

The Great Wave Harmed the United States

Roy Beck

Roy Beck argues in the following viewpoint that the high number of immigrants who came to America during the Great Wave of immigration between the 1880s and 1920s was unnecessary and harmful to American workers. The American frontier had already been conquered and large numbers of laborers were no longer needed. The continual arrival of tens of thousands of immigrants resulted in lower wages and prevented certain groups—particularly newly freed southern slaves—from obtaining well-paying jobs. In addition, Beck asserts, the immigrants' presence fostered hostility among American workers and encouraged feelings of racism and anti-Semitism. Beck is the Washington, D.C., editor of the *Social Contract* magazine and the author of *The Case Against Immigration*, from which the following viewpoint is excerpted.

Roy Beck, *The Case Against Immigration: The Moral, Economic, Social, and Environmental Reasons for Reducing U.S. Immigration Back to Traditional Levels*. New York: W.W. Norton, 1996. Copyright © 1996 by Roy Beck. Reproduced by permission.

In 1910, the fears of many Yankee settlers of Wausau, Wisconsin, came true. For years, they had worried that they would be overwhelmed by the German, Polish, and other immigrants pouring into town as part of what we now call the Great Wave of immigration. By 1910, the demographic takeover had occurred: immigrants and their children were in the majority. They changed the local culture, totally reversed the ruling political ideology, and by 1918 had taken over nearly every elected office in the county. Communities all across America similarly were caught in the social, economic, and political undertow of the Great Wave. Native-born Americans often felt like foreigners in their own hometowns, amidst a babel of foreign tongues and customs. For years, citizens clamored unsuccessfully for relief from Washington. Anti-immigrant hostilities and explosions of ethnic turmoil marred the society.

That is a different sort of history from the rose-colored views preached from many of the nation's political, media, and religious pulpits today: Americans are urged to turn from their opposition to today's levels of admissions and instead to "honor our nation's immigration tradition," as if that phrase describes a past in which Americans eagerly welcomed masses of immigrants. There are constant reminders that "we are an immigrant nation," that "we're all descended from immigrants," and that "immigration made our nation great." The *Chicago Sun-Times* reflected this view of history when it editorialized in 1994 that national policy must be consistent with "the country's historic openness toward immigration."

Legitimate Complaints About Immigration

For all of today's dewy-eyed remembrances of "tradition" and "openness," however, mass immigration always has provoked widespread, deep-rooted objections from much of the public. The historian John Higham of Johns Hopkins University detailed Americans' traditional anti-immigration sentiments in his seminal book, *Strangers in the Land* (1956), which is quoted often by immigration advocates who seek to show that restrictionists generally have been motivated by bigotry and irrational distrust of foreigners. But in the preface to his second edition and in subsequent writing, Higham emphasized that Americans also had some very legitimate reasons to campaign for immigration cuts.

One would never guess from most editorial writers and politicians today that there ever were legitimate complaints against immigration. They still speak of the Great Wave of 1880 to 1924 as a kind of golden era of immigration. Observing the congressional debate over immigration in the mid-1980s, University of California history professor Otis Graham wrote in *The Public Historian* that it was filled with remarks about what "history taught" but without anybody ever consulting a historian: "History was said to reveal a simple story, that mass immigration produced unalloyed benefits: economic growth and creative, law-abiding people like your grandparents and mine." While there was truth in those statements, they left out very important understandings about the costs that accompanied those benefits, he said.

Romanticized and sanitized by sentimental movies, novels, high school textbooks, stump speeches, and Fourth of July newspaper editorials, the Great Wave has been allowed to teach false lessons that have led present-day Americans to distorted positions on both sides of the immigration debate. . . .

Another View of the Great Wave

We have heard much about the warm personal stories of ancestors who came to America a century ago, but the hard realities and conflict brought by immigration must be restored to the picture if we are to learn anything helpful from the Great Wave experience. First, we must recognize that the Great Wave drew opposition from the beginning; there never was a period of broad public approval.

In 1880, the volume of annual immigration more than doubled over what it had been during each of the previous four years. And it was more than double the annual average of the previous sixty years. The Great Wave had begun. There was no fanfare or official declaration. Only later did Americans realize that something unprecedented was happening. There had been a surge like this in 1872–73 and back in 1854. But this surge was different. The 457,000 level of immigration in 1880 was not a peak but something of a floor for much of the next 44 years.

Many Americans agitated against the increased immigration almost immediately. Their anger was understandable. Manufacturers, such as the shoemaker Calvin T. Sampson of North Adams, Massachusetts, were importing foreign workers to fight the growing pressure from U.S. workers for an eight-hour workday and for other improvements in working conditions. Sounding remarkably like the pro-immigration forces of the 1990s, the industrialists of that time justified their actions on the basis of protecting an unfettered free-market system. They condemned labor organizing and strikes for better working conditions as violations of the "eternal laws of political economy," according to the historian Eric Foner.

Curbs on Immigration

Although American workers resented immigrants from both Europe and Asia, they gained their first success in 1882 with the Chinese Exclusion Act. The legislation and anti-immigrant hostilities leading to it included ugly racial overtones. But the special animus against the Chinese immigrants also was driven by the egregious use of them for several years as strikebreakers. In California, the imported Chinese workers had come to make up a quarter of the wage force even before the Great Wave began.

The pressure to cut immigration did not stop with the action against the Chinese. By 1885, Congress was persuaded to move against some of the immigration from Europe. The Alien Contract Law halted the practice of companies contracting to transport immigrants who then were legally bound to work in indentured servitude for at least a year and often for several years.

Those measures knocked the numbers down some. But the volume remained high. John Higham says there was widespread public demand for more curbs on immigration in 1886, the year of the dedication of the Statue of Liberty. Many otherwise well-informed people today have misconstrued that event, suggesting that the statue was placed in New York City's harbor as a sign of welcome to the new wave of immigrants. In fact, the statue and its symbolism had absolutely nothing to do with immigration, as the museum inside the statue makes abundantly clear. It was only coincidence that the statue was placed at a time and place where millions of immigrants were entering the United States. Given the deep opposition to the increased immigration numbers at the time, it is doubtful that the people of New York would have contributed the money to build the pedestal if they had thought the statue, which officially was entitled *Liberty Enlightening the World*, had been intended as *America Inviting the World*.

American Workers Were Shut Out

While the rapid industrialization of the northern economy created openings for many new wage earners, the country did not require hundreds of thousands of foreign workers to meet that need. Large numbers of rural Americans, especially white and black workers in the war-ravaged South, could have taken many of those new northern jobs. But most were shut out of the opportunity by the Great Wave immigrants from Europe. The economist Joshua L. Rosenbloom of the University of Kansas found that immigrants were able to use ethnic networking as a means to fill job openings with workers from their own nationality groups. Like many employers in the 1990s, once northern companies learned that they could easily fill their jobs through immigrant networking, they made few efforts to attract new supplies of American workers. "Only when European immigration was cut off during the First World War were concerted efforts undertaken to develop the machinery necessary to attract low-wage southern workers," Rosenbloom concluded.

The most tragic result of the manufacturers' preference for immigrant labor was a half-century postponement of opportunity for most of the freed slaves to seek higher-paying jobs outside of the South. That left a large percentage of them dependent for jobs from the very class of southerners that previously had enslaved them. The Great Wave began just as the federal government had abandoned Reconstruction and had withdrawn federal troops from the South. With the immigration-filled northern industries having no need of their services and the federal government no longer willing to protect their rights, many black workers were trapped in the South where most of their political and economic gains since the Civil War were stripped away.

Meanwhile, native-born white Americans in the North and West were feeling their own effects of the greatly expanded pool of labor. One reason the industrialists were so eager to enlarge the labor supply was to try to flatten American wage rates, which were far higher than wages in Europe. Because of an abundance of underutilized natural resources (especially open land) and a relatively small population, the New World in 1870 paid wages that were 136 percent higher than in the heavily populated Old World. But by 1913, American workers had lost almost half that pay advantage, after decades of massive additions of foreign workers. Immigrant labor depressed wages for native labor by competing directly on almost equal terms, according to the economists Timothy J. Hatton and Jeffrey G. Williamson, in their book *Migration and the International Labor Market 1850–1939*. They state that the immigrants "marginalized" most native women and black workers, keeping them out of the mainstream of industrial jobs.

Adding to Americans' concerns about the labor competition from immigrants was the psychological shock of being informed in 1890 by the U.S. Census Bureau that so many people had settled in the West that the frontier, under the Census definition, no longer existed. Williamson has written that, around that time, the absorptive capacity of the American labor market declined; thereafter, immigration dragged down wages even more than it had during the early part of the Great Wave.

Conditions Had Changed

At that point, it didn't matter what proportion of the population immigration had once been; conditions had changed. The country had reached a level of maturity that no longer needed or could handle immigration at the old proportions or numbers. Frederick Jackson Turner, the most famous of the country's chroniclers of the closing of the frontier, found immigration much more threatening than during a time of open land. He wrote in the *Chicago Record-Herald* for 25 September 1901:

> The immigrant of the preceding period was assimilated with comparative ease, and it can hardly be doubted that valuable contributions to American character have come from this infusion of non-English stock into the American people. But the free lands that made the process of absorption easy have gone. The immigration is becoming increasingly more difficult of assimilation. Its competition with American labor un-

der existing conditions may give increased power to the pro-
ducer, but the effects upon American well-being are dangerous in the extreme.

Congress Acts

A heightened sense of urgency drove Americans to insist on deci-
sive action in Washington. On 9 February 1897, the U.S. House
of Representatives began a dramatic series of legislative events: (1)
The House voted 217 to 36 to approve an immigrant literacy test.
That test would have significantly curtailed the immigration of
the next decades. (2) A week later, the Senate voted 34 to 31 to
send the immigration restriction bill to President Grover Cleveland. (3) Cleveland vetoed it on March 2. (4) The next day, the
House overrode the veto by 195 to 37. (5) The Senate—having
earlier approved it by such a narrow margin—did not bother to
attempt a two-thirds override of the veto. Thus the Great Wave
narrowly escaped being shut off after only seventeen years and before it grew to its greatest strength.

Restrictionism had failed for the moment. There were no public opinion polls to record the actual attitudes of the American
people. But the majority of their representatives in Congress
worked for the next twenty-seven years to reduce legal immigration levels. That suggests a large segment of Americans who
wanted to substantially change the spectacle on Ellis Island where
hundreds of thousands of immigrants a year lined up to be pro-
cessed into the U.S. labor force.

The restrictionist issue carried over to the next presidential election. William McKinley, running on a platform that supported
restriction, was victorious; this time there would be no presidential veto protecting the foreign influx. But while the Senate voted
45-28 in 1898 to stop the Great Wave, a reconstituted House narrowly defeated the restriction, 104 to 101. If two members had
switched from "no" to "yes," the Great Wave would have lost
much of its volume. And the peak decade for Ellis Island never
would have occurred.

One branch or the other of Congress was in nearly constant mo-
tion during the next two decades, trying to stop the Great Wave.
The majority of the members of the U.S. House of Representa-

tives voted to restrain immigration in 1897, 1902, 1906, 1912, 1913, 1915, 1916, 1917, 1921, and 1924. The Senate did the same in 1897, 1898, 1912, 1915, 1916, 1917, 1921, and 1924. But for years, the supporters of high immigration always were able to persuade a president to veto restrictionist legislation and managed to win just enough votes in one of the houses of Congress to prevent a two-thirds vote to override a veto. Industrialists lobbied hard to protect their supply of cheap labor. And leaders of growing blocs of newly naturalized immigrant citizens were influential in making sure immigration continued to add more people to their ethnic power bases.

The Social Fabric Frays

The country paid high costs for the delay in enacting restrictions. John Higham—who continues to believe that immigration generally has strengthened the American character—has warned defenders of the current wave of immigration that they risk repeating the disastrous mistakes of those who early [in the twentieth] century insisted on keeping the Great Wave going. "The inescapable need for some rational control over the volume of immigration in an increasingly crowded world was plain to see, then as now," he wrote. But the business interests, the immigrant leaders, and the traditionalists who feared any increase in the powers of government blocked all reform and allowed problems to fester and grow. As another 14 million immigrants entered between 1897 and 1917, the social fabric frayed, as exemplified by the upheaval in Wausau, Wisconsin. Frustrations among Americans overflowed. America endured a nationwide spread of intense anti-Semitism, anti-immigrant hysteria, and the heyday of the new Ku Klux Klan as a "nationwide, all-purpose vigilante movement," according to Higham.

It was that extreme reaction to the extreme volume of immigration that has tended to cause immigration restrictionists today to be suspect as right-wing racists. But Otis Graham of the University of California, Santa Barbara, has noted that "Restrictionism attracted some of the best minds in America, including many liberal clergymen, spokesmen for organized labor and the black community, and socialists."

Part of the concern of the liberal restrictionists was the abominable conditions for many immigrants. A congressional study found that new arrivals were three times more likely than natives to be on welfare in 1909; immigrants comprised more than half the people on welfare nationwide. Chicago was especially hard-hit; four out of every five welfare recipients at that time were immigrants and their children. Foreign-born residents constituted a third of the patients in public hospitals and insane asylums in the country. The situation was worse in New York City, where the president of the board of health said that almost half the expenditures were for the immigrant poor.

A national commission studied the impact of immigration for five years and concluded in 1911 that it was contributing to low wages and poor working conditions. It was not until 1917, however, that immigration restrictions finally were enacted into law as the House (287-106) and the Senate (62-19) overrode President Wilson's second veto.

In the public's view, the 1917 action did not block enough immigrants. Another act in 1921 set a numerical ceiling for the first time. And then in 1924, Congress decisively gave the American people the respite they so long had sought. The "Great Aberration" was over, after forty-four years.

CHAPTER 3

The Golden Door Begins to Close

✺ Chapter Preface

Immigration into the United States was relatively free of restrictions during the nation's first century. Immigrants were desperately needed to settle and build the young country. Furthermore, the U.S. Constitution was unclear about whether the responsibility for regulating immigration belonged to the states or the federal government. The Alien and Sedition Acts—which made it more difficult for immigrants to become citizens and permitted the deportation of anyone who criticized the government, president, or Congress—were passed by Congress in 1798 but expired two years later. In 1819 Congress passed its first significant law concerning immigration. The law required all immigrants to provide their name, age, and occupation when entering the United States, and in 1820 the United States began keeping records of immigrants entering America.

Following the Civil War (1861–1865), labor unions began agitating for laws restricting immigration. The new arrivals were usually willing to work for less pay than established American workers, thereby displacing "natives" from their jobs and driving down wages for all. Restrictions on immigration started slowly; in 1875 Congress first prohibited prostitutes and convicted criminals from immigrating. Later, Congress added paupers, the mentally ill, polygamists (directed at Mormons), and those with a "loathsome or contagious" disease to the prohibited list. In 1882, Congress passed the first law that banned immigrants based on their ethnicity—the Chinese Exclusion Act—which effectively cut off immigration from China. The bill was passed in response to labor union fears that Chinese immigrants, who numbered about one hundred thousand at the time, threatened the American economy because they were willing to work at dangerous jobs and for less pay than American workers. Although these restrictions did little to limit the number of European immigrants, they did establish a precedent of restricting those immigrants deemed to be dangerous to the health of the nation.

Perhaps the most important attempt at restriction was the literacy test. Beginning in the 1880s, opponents of unlimited immigration began supporting the idea that immigrants over the age of sixteen must be able to read between thirty and forty words in their own language. A large percentage of the "new immigrants" were from southern and eastern Europe. Anti-immigration activists sought to limit immigration from these regions. Because many of these immigrants were illiterate, the literacy test was seen as a way to prevent them from entering the United States without seeming blatantly racist. Bills featuring a literacy test for new immigrants appeared in Congress thirty-nine times over twenty-five years. The bills passed in either the House or the Senate seven times, and passed in both houses three times, but they were vetoed by Presidents Grover Cleveland, Howard Taft, and Woodrow Wilson. Congress finally rallied enough support to override President Wilson's veto in 1917.

Now that Congress had successfully passed the literacy test as a means to exclude certain immigrants, it turned its sights to drastically reducing the number of immigrants admitted to the United States. In 1921 it passed a quota law. Although it did not exclude any nationalities, the law strictly limited the number of immigrants from any one country. The law established a quota for each country based on the percentage of that country's population living in the United States according to the 1910 census. The quota law was amended in 1924 to use the census figures of 1890, since the composition of the population at that time consisted of a larger number of races deemed desirable—in other words, white, Anglo-Saxon, and Protestant.

The laws restricting immigration were extremely controversial at the time, but it wasn't until four decades later than the 1965 Immigration Act created a quota system that no longer favored immigrants from northern and western Europe. The authors in the following chapter examine the debate over restrictions on immigration to the United States.

Viewpoint 1

"If this Chinese tide be allowed to keep flowing in, it will corrupt still more our ethnological hell-broth, and add another and a notable element of disturbance."

Immigrant Chinese Laborers Must Be Excluded

E.W. Gilliam

E.W. Gilliam was a nineteenth-century professor who wrote about the threat to the white American worker from Chinese workers and Africans. In this excerpt from an 1886 article, Gilliam discusses how Chinese immigrants are pouring out of China and establishing new colonies all over the world. The number of Chinese immigrants in Christian nations increased over 400 percent in just a few years. The history of their migration, he points out, demonstrates what a threat Chinese immigration could be to the United States if it is not controlled.

Gilliam argues in the following viewpoint that the United States is an attractive destination for Chinese immigrants. Wages are high and the cost of living is relatively cheap. The Chinese laborers, known as "coolies," work harder and for less money than American workers; thus, their presence endangers

E.W. Gilliam, "Chinese Immigration," *North American Review*, July 1886.

the livelihood of white American workers. Even if the Chinese come to the United States only to earn money and then return to China, their thrifty nature ensures that America will be bled of substantial wealth. Therefore, Gilliam asserts, it is imperative that Chinese laborers be prohibited from immigrating to the United States.

For centuries European communication with "far Cathay" [China] was checked by the length and difficulty of the way. Embassies from the Roman emperors and the mediæval popes occasionally reached this distant land. Subsequently, trade concessions were grudgingly granted to certain European nations, and Christian missionaries allowed entrance. Their aggressive teachings, won martyrdom. The missions vanished in blood, and China, with a bang, shut fast her door against Western "barbarians."

Meanwhile, her dealings had been with rude peoples, to whom she was vastly superior. For fifteen centuries she was a teacher; all other nations having real intercourse with her were pupils; and, indeed, during the period of mediæval Europe, China unquestionably was the most civilized country on earth. Under these circumstances was developed an intense national pride—a further source of exclusiveness. It finds expression in all of China's popular names, which represent her as being at the center, while around and far beyond her borders lie the "barbarian" countries—such as "Central Flower," "Central Flowery Land," "Middle Kingdom."

But Europe advanced splendidly, and the present century found the Asiatic possessions of three of its most powerful nations encircling the empire, save on its coast line—Russia, on the north and west; England, on the south-west; and France, on the south. Complications arose, and China felt forced to alter her foreign policy. Diplomatic intercourse with the states of Christendom, and commercial relations upon a treaty basis, were the outcome of the opium war with England (1839–42). China suddenly threw open to the trade of the world five of her most important ports; a migratory spirit has been aroused, and a tide is pouring through the gates of this colossal empire. To other peoples, indeed, China remains practically an unknown land. Some missionaries and a few explorers are found in the interior; but the money-loving Chinese are streaming over the world, and quietly establishing themselves, and forming colonies after their fashion, in the trade centers of Christendom.

The Chinese Swarm

There are 500,000 in the Malay Archipelago, and 1,500,000 in Siam [Thailand]. Singapore is the distributing point, whence vast numbers annually go into the adjacent countries. The immigration, in 1882, was 100,000; in 1883, 150,000; and an increase was expected the following year. Singapore is itself overrun with them, and illustrates their shrewdness in seizing upon trade centers. Situated on the straits of Malacca, at the extremity of the Malay peninsula, the touching point for every east-bound steamship, and back, it has risen to great importance. The Chinese have swarmed into it.

"On my first visit to Singapore, in 1871," writes Baron von Hubner, "the population consisted of 100 white families, 20,000 Malays, and a few thousand Chinese. On my return there, in the beginning of 1884, the population stood 100 white families, 20,000 Malays, and 86,000 Chinese. A new Chinese town had sprung up, with magnificent stores, and beautiful residences and pagodas. I imagined that I was transported to Canton."

Since 1860, 200,000 have entered Chili and Peru—an immense number when one considers the small European population. There are 130,000 in Cuba. They are pressing into the Sandwich Islands. There are 50,000 in Australia, and more than three times this number in the United States—30,000 being in San Francisco, where they constitute one-seventh of the population, and one-fourth of the laboring class; and, spite of prohibitory laws, they steadily increase, in these countries, in numbers and influence, finding a way to us through Mexico and British Columbia.

These are recent facts, and, whatever may be the past history of the Chinese, they demonstrate a present powerful migratory movement.

The cause is not political oppression. China theoretically is a despotism, and its officials are often cruel and corrupt; yet powerful local correctives exist, and, upon the whole, the Chinese are the freest native people of Asia.

Nor does the cause wholly lie in the pressure of super-dense population. There are immense fertile districts in Manchooria sparsely peopled; and though Mongolia is largely desert, yet there remain many broad unoccupied areas, susceptible of cultivation, and which once supported the warriors of Genghis Khan. Throughout the empire the population to the square mile is but 90; in China proper, 180. There are, doubtless, swarming coast districts where it averages from 300 to 500, where agriculture has been pushed to the extreme limits of possibility, and the struggle for existence is intense.

This migratory movement has its mainspring in the Chinaman's wish to better his condition; and a number of considerations combine to encourage the flow specially toward our shores.

In no civilized country are wages so high and living (relatively) so cheap, as in the United States: in none are wages so low as in China. A workingman in California receives from $3 to $5 per day; in China, from 10 cents to 16 cents. If we consider, then, that on opposite shores of the same ocean are two countries, in one of which wages are at the maximum, in the other at the minimum; that the one has a sparse population, the other a population remarkably dense; that America's climate is congenial, and her government liberal; that competition has reduced the passage as low, in some instances, as $12, and that, under the "contract system," by which a mortgage is given upon his future wages, the poorest Chinaman may emigrate—we have the conditions that naturally stimulate the Chinese toward us.

The magnitude of the possible inflow is appalling. The empire covers a third of Asia, and holds a third of the world's inhabitants. China proper has a homogeneous population of 360,000,000. A migratory movement in such a race toward a given point, is startling in the extreme; and unless we are satisfied, as a recent writer states it, that the greatest possible influx would do us no harm, it is wisdom to meet any danger at the outset.

As far as Chinese immigration is transient merely, it may exist to such a degree as to justify exclusion on this account alone. If the Chinaman comes only to accumulate and transfer, we may be disastrously bled. The scale of wages and living is so low in China, that what we regard as a small sum makes a fortune there; and the impulse of the poor Chinese, whose lot in their own land is often extremely hard, to go abroad where wages are high, and return with the few thousands that bring affluence and ease, is powerful. Vast numbers are acting on this impulse. The Chinese in Australia return annually to China, in gold-dust alone, a quarter million of dollars. A statement appears that the remittance from California last year was $15,000,000, and that the sum total for twenty-five years has been little short of $200,000,000! . . .

Chinese Accomplishments

In California their success has been phenomenal. An inferior class (generally) of Chinese workmen, under the immense disadvantage of not knowing our language, on knowing it imperfectly, without experience as teamsters or in the use of agricultural machinery, against race prejudice and the powerful opposition of trade-unions—they are now in more than successful competition with Americans in every article of necessity and luxury. Accustomed, in their native rice fields, to stand all day with the feet in water and the head exposed to an almost tropical sun, they have dyked thousands of acres of the tule and tide-water lands—accomplishing a work from whose rough and unhealthful character the ordinary American shrank. They have taken worn-out and abandoned mines, and profitably worked them. In field and vineyard they are unexcelled as laborers. Along the Pacific Railroad they have displaced white section-hands. The Rocky Mountain coal mines and other mines of that region have become, in many instances, Chinese settlements.

In San Francisco they are the only professional embroiderers, and already control a number of industries. Last year, in "Chinatown" alone, nearly 3,000 were employed in the manufacture of all kinds of clothing, boots and shoes, leather, cigars, etc., etc. They use the best modern machinery, and, quick-handed and intelligent, rapidly become adepts. The Hop Kee Shoe Company, on Dupont Street, at certain seasons of the year, employ 300 men. Their goods largely supply the Pacific coast, and now find a market as far east as Salt Lake City. In the manufacture of clothing, shirts, ladies' underwear, etc., 1,245 sewing-machines were used, and with marvelous dexterity and diligence. These industries are constantly increasing. An American manufacturer, as a recent writer points out, employs Chinese workmen at low rates. Other manufacturers are soon compelled to do the same. Presently rich Chinamen appear who buy out the manufacturers, and the entire business becomes "Chinese."

A Lower Standard of Living

The cause is patent. The American, with stronger physique, and more inventive, if less imitative, power, is, so far forth, a better workman. But a Chinaman can live on a fourth of what is required by the average American, exercising rigid rules of thrift and economy. He can, therefore, easily underbid the American, and will always so far do so as to control the situation. The man who will do the work for half the sum, is in universal demand. The American must either lower his wage, or leave.

But it would require the same training of centuries, and under populous conditions unknown to us, for the American to come down to the Chinaman's reduced standard of comfort. Even could he at once descend to it, it would be undesirable. Low wages, with temporary local advantage to manufacturers, would ultimately prove an enduring national curse. Their incidental influence upon production is adverse, in making the laborer less efficient, and diminishing the tendency toward improved economic methods.

Their proper and permanent effect, however, is upon distribution, in giving to capital a larger share of the wealth, and widening the gap between poor and rich—an evil already assuming among us threatening aspects.

In judging Chinese immigration, we distinguish between the "water rats" of Canton and Hong Kong—the opium-smoking, hard-looking, criminal scum of seaport cities—and the clean, bright-eyed, well-bred Chinamen from the interior rice and tea farms, raised in homes where parents exact obedience and children yield it. There are, too, doubtless, noble spirits among the Chinese, many whom the best of us could admire and love. But these come not to us.

A Blight on the Pacific Coast

The main-stream upon California has been vile. Beyond question it is blighting the Pacific coast. The Californians are the most competent judges, and their opinion, excepting some interested manufacturers, is intense and unanimous. The State is said to be approaching retrogression, and even her millionaires are "gravitating" eastward. We have before us the "Report of the Special Committee of the Board of Supervisors of San Francisco, on the Condition of the Chinese quarter," issued last July [1885]. The facts to which they testify, after a personal and most painstaking inspection, including affidavits from prominent physicians and law officers, can scarcely be questioned. They affirm:

That in 12 blocks are crowded, in indescribable filth, 30,000 men, and 1,385 women, of the latter 57 being legitimate wives, 567 professional prostitutes, the residue either concubines or women of doubtful character; that, beds being unknown, they sleep in bunks, with two in a bunk, "relays" in daytime, and rolls of bedding for sleeping on floors, women and children being stuck in out-of-the-way corners; that there are 150 gambling dives, the approaches to which are generally so barricaded as to defy police detection; that, while there is an "opium lay-out" in nearly every sleeping-room, the public resorts are 26, with 319 bunks; that there are 35 dens of white prostitution, generally patronized by Chinese, and 69 of Chinese prostitution, patronized generally by whites; that among the latter especially the rates are extremely low, and that white boys, as young as even 8 or 10, are often enticed into them; that there is no city in the world where so many children are afflicted with secret diseases as San Francisco, and that nine-tenths of it is traceable to the excessively cheap prostitution of "Chinatown"; that the Chinese prostitutes are regularly bought and sold for terms of years, and that organized bodies of villains exist, as the Ye Tung Society, for the purpose of capturing and restoring to the owner fugitive prostitutes; that gambling, opium-smoking, and prostitution are so intrenched that the police force necessary to suppress them would bankrupt the city; that the course of justice is systematically baffled by the powerful guilds or secret tribunals; that, within these 12 blocks, there are 13 Joss Houses [a place of worship], where hideous idols squat upon the altars; and that for every Chinaman's soul rationally converted, scores of American souls are lost through the increase of vice.

America for Americans!

A purer stream of immigration, while lessening these moral evils, would enhance danger on the economic side.

Therefore, Congress, in 1882—as Australia has done—imposed restrictions upon immigration. As these have proven inadequate, effectual measures should be taken, or conflicts will be inevitable. The California feeling is spreading. Those who know China, know her friendship should be cherished; nevertheless, we must be self-protecting. Traditions to the winds, that do not make America first of all for Americans!

An uppermost thought in the political mind of the age is the national importance of homogeneous population. Its absence, even within the circumscribed area of those white varieties of the race, whose language, laws, and religion have a common origin, is today vexing England to the core, and stimulating Bismarck in a course toward the Poles that is brutal, yet sagacious. Many think we Americans have had enough of immigration, even of our own color. The riotous tendencies among us largely come from the foreign element. America's digestive powers are strained to assimilate it, and develop within it that organizing principle which is the Anglo-Saxon's glory. The Negro question, too, remains unsolved. The race has a phenomenal fecundity, and should and must remain distinct, or our descendants will be hybrids inferior to the native negro ancestry. Should the race become vagabond and moribund, it would poison the body politic, and drag down those with whom it is allied. Should it advance intellectually, race struggles are foreshadowed. If this Chinese tide be allowed to keep flowing in, it will corrupt still more our ethnological hell-broth, and add another and a notable element of disturbance. The three great families into which mankind is divided—black, yellow, white—(the debasing effects of amalgamation across color lines indicate this) should develop *within themselves*, and toward what apparently are their respective bounds, a half-civilized, civilized, and enlightened condition.

Viewpoint 2

"The white man of California . . . gets a larger wage to-day, probably, than he would if the Chinese were not present. At the same time the labors of the Chinese reduce the cost for him of all the necessaries of life."

Chinese Immigration Benefits America

George F. Seward

George F. Seward served as the U.S. minister to China from 1876 to 1880. In the following viewpoint, Seward maintains that the Chinese who immigrate to the United States are freemen, not slaves or indentured servants, as some allege. The Chinese work for whomever they please, and whenever and wherever they please. Seward also argues that Chinese immigrants are not responsible for white unemployment; in California, where the Chinese are most numerous, wages are higher than in other parts of the country, which indicates that there is an inadequate supply of labor to meet demand. He further asserts that Chinese immigration has benefited the United States. Chinese workers have started businesses that were nonexistent before their arrival. Seward also maintains that, given the chance, the Chinese assimilate easily into American culture. He does not believe that the United States is threatened by an imminent Chinese immigration invasion.

George F. Seward, "Mongolian Immigration," *North American Review*, June 1882.

It is said that the Chinese in this country are not freemen, and that it is not just to our people to force upon them competition with a servile class.

Not Slaves or Contract Laborers

It is clear that we should not tolerate a servile class among us. I contend, however, that Chinese labor, as it is seen in this country, is not servile.

It is an admitted fact that no slave-holding, rightly so called, is known in China. It is an admitted fact that no Chinaman in this country has appealed to the courts to be freed from a condition of slavery. Under these circumstances, those who allege that Chinese labor is servile have fallen back upon the proposition that the Chinese come to us under a contract system, which is a modified form of slavery.

But of this there is no proof. If contracts are made, under which the lenders of money control laborers, there should be no difficulty in demonstrating the fact. In all the history of the anti-Chinese agitation, not one such contract has been produced, saving only in the case of prostitutes, and no evidence has been given as of knowledge proving the fact. . . .

I do not assert that Chinese who are proposing to come to this country do not borrow money in China and agree to repay it out of their earnings here. This practice prevails among immigrants from all countries, but it does not create nor imply servile labor. It shows simply that a given person has the capacity to contract as a freeman, and that the lender expects his client to behave as an honest freeman should.

As a matter of fact, evidence taken in California proves that the Chinese in this country are controlled by no masters. They take service when, where, and with whom they please. They leave service when it suits them to do so. They are almost as exacting in these respects as are the other laborers of the country.

Wages Are Higher in California

It is said again that they displace white laborers.

The laboring man in the communities of the Pacific coast sees Chinamen at work all around him. He sees also, sometimes, if not

often, white men who are not at work. It is natural for him to believe, under these circumstances, that the Chinese are getting the
wages which white men would command if the Chinese were ab-
sent. He has found wages tending to fall, and it is natural for him
to judge that this tendency results from the competition of Asiatics. This simple way of looking at the matter may be very incor-
rect, nevertheless.

It is well known that wages are higher in California than elsewhere in America, and herein lies the proof that there has been no
ruinous competition between the two races. An over-supply of labor causes low wages; an inadequate supply may cause high wages.
The laboring man may argue the case in whatever way and with
whatever sincerity, but the facts decide the question.

The Chinese Provide Valuable Services and Labor

There are some directions in which Chinese labor controls the
market in California, but Chinamen have not displaced white men
even in these directions. They make cigars. None to speak of were
made in California until the Chinese took up the trade. They make
shoes. None were made before they began the business. They wash
clothes. As a rule, it is the clothing of white mechanics and laborers and of their families. They do a great deal of the work of
railroad-building and of reclaiming swamp lands. The supply of
white laborers has been inadequate in both directions.

It should be remembered, also, that the Chinese have made possible industries which could not have been undertaken in their absence, and which have given larger opportunities to our own
people. We occupy the territory made available by the railroads
which have been constructed with the assistance of Chinamen.
We till the swamp lands reclaimed by them. We own the mills and
larger factories in which they work, and the sum of the wages of
our people who are employed is far away in excess of those of the
Chinese operatives.

That wages should tend to fall in California was to be expected.
They were far higher than elsewhere in our country, and still are.
The influx of population must necessarily work a change in this
respect. But the white man of California is raised in the scale of

industry by the presence of the Chinese, and he gets a larger wage to-day, probably, than he would if the Chinese were not present. At the same time the labors of the Chinese reduce the cost for him of all the necessaries of life.

The Chinese and Their Wages

It is urged, further, that Chinamen send their wages out of the country.

The Chinaman wears good clothing and eats good food when he can afford to do so. He is not so far a slave to the habits of his ancestors as to wear a suit of cotton cloth and sandals of straw when he can do better, nor eat rice when a fuller diet is available. The conditions of climate and of labor among us are so far different from those in South China, that better clothes and better food become indispensable. As a matter of fact, the Chinese in California dress better than other laborers, and eat quite as good food.

It follows that the Chinese, like most other people, live well up to their incomes. I do not believe that they are able to send out of the country more than ten per cent. of their wages. The advantage of the other ninety per centum remains with us. They create much wealth and carry away a small portion of it only. . . .

The Chinese Do Assimilate

A further and very positive declaration is that the Chinese will not assimilate with our people; that they do not care to become citizens; that they are not fit to become citizens; that our civilization makes no impress upon them; that they remain, and will remain forever, an alien and indigested element in our body politic.

Perhaps no misstatement which has been put in circulation in regard to the much-abused Chinaman has been more often repeated or has found more ready acceptance than this; yet it is as unfounded as it would be to declare that one earth does not nourish him and us; one heaven does not overarch his race and ours. The Chinaman does assimilate with us when we allow him to do so. . . .

If they do not assimilate, in what do they not? It is admitted that they take up with our industries. It is admitted that they are keen merchants and traders. It is admitted that they learn our language quickly. It is admitted that many join our churches. Their dress in our country is a mixture of their own and ours, they live in our kind of houses, they eat our food, they follow us, in fact, about as fast and as far as we allow them to follow.

There Is Merit in the Chinese

I have no patience with the statement that the Chinaman is a different sort of being from ourselves. I do not agree with Senator Miller when he says that one person like Washington or Newton, Franklin or Lincoln, has been of more service to humanity than all the Chinese who have lived and died in the lands of the Hoang-ho. Sir Frederick Bruce knew them, and said that the members of the cabinet of Peking were fit to be compared with those of any Western cabinet. . . . Why does the study of the literature of China fascinate all who enter upon it? Why has China had a settled government far longer than any other race or people?

There is merit in the Chinese stock, and those who do not see the fact do not know them or are blinded by prejudice. Having merit, they would become a valuable accession to our society if we would allow them. They were far away ahead of us in the arts and sciences, and in the refinements of life, a few generations ago. We must not claim that our stock is a better one now, unless we are prepared to admit that theirs was a better one then.

Not Likely to Overwhelm Us

A further objection urged against the Chinese as immigrants is that they are likely to overwhelm us; that their numbers and necessities are great, and that they will fall upon our shores in such force as to take possession of all our employments, and leave us no room and breathing space.

I should not like to see such a condition of things, but I am aware of no reason why it may be expected. If the history of their race gave one instance in which they have occupied the territory of men of Caucasian origin, I might feel differently. So far are they from having done this that they have left intact the boundaries even of their Asiatic neighbors. They do not come among us in considerable numbers. In thirty years they have given to the Pacific coast less than one hundred thousand people, while we of the Eastern States and of Europe have poured in there at least one million. They do not hold their ratio in the population, but are becoming less numerous in relation to the whole.

It will be time enough to deal with this danger when it arrives. To-day it is not a danger at all. An Eastern man may smile at the fears of Californians when he sees eight hundred thousand Europeans arriving in New York as against ten or a dozen thousand Chinese at San Francisco; a million, perhaps, to reënforce fifty millions against ten thousand to reënforce one hundred thousand.

Other objections have been urged against the Chinese, some of which are unfounded and others are more or less just. Among the former are such statements as that they have set up a government of their own upon our soil, that they would not fight for us in time of war, etc. Among the latter are the declarations that the few Chinese women in this country are in large part prostitutes, that many criminals find immunity by escaping to our shores, and that some diseased persons and paupers come among us. I shall not stop to disprove the first of these allegations, nor do more here than to say that while there are evils in the latter directions, the tendency in California has been to draw a darker picture than the facts warrant. . . .

Unfounded Claims

Those who hold that Chinese labor is servile, that the Chinese displace laborers of our own stock, that they send their earnings out of the country, that they are vicious, that they will not assimilate with us, that they are destined to overrun our country, having asserted all these things, take it for granted that all men must agree in their conclusion that the Chinese should be excluded from among us.

That the statements of fact put forward by these persons are largely unfounded is shown, as I believe, in the evidence and considerations which have been briefly summarized in . . . this paper.

Viewpoint 3

"The importance of illiteracy among aliens is overestimated."

The Literacy Test Does Not Detect Superior Character

Charles Nagel

Charles Nagel was the U.S. secretary of commerce and labor from 1909 to 1913. The following viewpoint is an extract of a letter written by Nagel on February 12, 1913, to President William H. Taft concerning a bill passed by Congress to require a literacy test for new immigrants. The bill required that the male head of household be able to read in his native language, although his wife or minor children were not required to be literate. Nagel argues that these provisions are impractical and without merit. According to the new law, a family in which the children and mother could read would be turned away if the father could not read. Nagel concludes that requiring a literacy test does not ensure the quality of immigrants to the United States. Taft vetoed the bill requiring a literacy test for immigrants; however, the bill was finally passed by Congress in 1917 despite President Woodrow Wilson's veto.

Charles Nagel, letter to William H. Taft, February 12, 1913.

On the 4th [of February 1913], Mr. Hilles, by your direction, sent me Senate Bill 3175, "An act to regulate the immigration of aliens to and the residence of aliens in the United States," with the request that I inform you at my earliest convenience if I know of any objection to its approval. I now return the bill with my comments. . . .

With respect to the literacy test I feel compelled to state . . . in my opinion, this is a provision of controlling importance, not only because of the immediate effect which it may have upon immigration, and the embarrassment and cost it may impose upon the service, but because it involves a principle of far-reaching consequence with respect to which your attitude will be regarded with profound interest.

The Bill's Provisions

The provision as it now appears will require careful reading. In some measure the group system is adopted—that is, one qualified immigrant may bring in certain members of his family—but the effect seems to be that a qualified alien may bring in members of his family who may themselves be disqualified; whereas a disqualified member would exclude all dependent members of his family no matter how well qualified they might otherwise be. In other words, a father who can read a dialect might bring in an entire family of absolutely illiterate people, barring his sons over sixteen years of age, whereas a father who can not read a dialect would bring about the exclusion of his entire family, although every one of them can read and write.

Furthermore, the distinction in favor of the female members of the family as against the male members does not seem to me to rest upon sound reason. Sentimentally, of course, it appeals, but industrially considered it does not appear to me that the distinction is sound. Furthermore, there is no provision for the admission of aliens who have been domiciled here and who have simply gone abroad for a visit. The test would absolutely exclude them upon return.

Negative Aspects of the Bill

In the administration of this law, very considerable embarrassment will be experienced. This at least is the judgment of members of the immigration force upon whose recommendations I rely. Delay will necessarily ensue at all ports, but on the borders of Canada and Mexico that delay will almost necessarily result in great friction and constant complaint. Furthermore, the force will have to be very considerably increased, and the appropriation will probably be in excess of present sums expended by as much as a million dollars.

The force of interpreters will have to be largely increased and, practically speaking, the bureau will have to be in a position to have an interpreter for any kind of language or dialect of the world at any port at any time. Finally, the interpreters will necessarily be foreigners, and with respect to only a very few of the languages or dialects will it be possible for the officials in charge to exercise anything like supervision.

I am of the opinion that this provision cannot be defended upon its merits. It was originally urged as a selective test. For some time, recommendations in its support upon that ground have been brought to our attention. The matter has been considered from that point of view, and I became completely satisfied that upon that ground the test could not be sustained. The older argument is now abandoned, and in the later conferences, at least, the ground is taken that the provision is to be defended as a practical measure to exclude a large proportion of undesirable immigrants from certain countries. The measure proposes to reach its results by indirection and is defended purely upon the ground of practical policy, the final purpose being to reduce the quantity of cheap labor in this country.

I cannot accept this argument. No doubt the law would exclude a considerable percentage of immigration from southern Italy, among the Poles, the Mexicans, and the Greeks. This exclusion would embrace probably in large part undesirable but also a great many desirable people, and the embarrassment, expense, and distress to those who seek to enter would be out of all proportion to any good that can possibly be promised for this measure.

My observation leads me to the conclusion that so far as the merits of the individual immigrant are concerned the test is altogether overestimated. The people who come from the countries named are frequently illiterate because opportunities have been denied them. The oppression with which these people have to contend in modern times is not religious, but it cosists of a denial of the opportunity to acquire reading and writing. Frequently the attempts to learn to read and write the language of the particular people is discouraged by the government, and these immigrants in coming to our shores are really striving to free themselves from the conditions under which they have been compelled to live.

America Needs Workers

So far as the industrial conditions are concerned, I think the question has been superficially considered. We need labor in this country, and the natives are unwilling to do the work which the aliens come over to do. It is perfectly true that in a few cities and localities there are congested conditions. It is equally true that in very much larger areas we are practically without help. In my judgment, no sufficiently earnest and intelligent effort has been made to bring our wants and our supply together, and so far the same forces that give the chief support to this provision of the new bill have stubornly resisted any effort looking to an intelligent distribution of new immigration to meet the needs of our vast country. In my judgment, no such drastic measure based upon a ground which is untrue and urged for a reason which we are unwilling to assert should be adopted until we have at least exhausted the possibilities of a rational distribution of these new forces.

The Immigrants' Character

Furthermore, there is a misapprehension as to the character of the people who come over here to remain. It is true that in certain localities newly arrived aliens live under deplorable conditions. Just as much may be said of certain localities that have been inhabited for a hundred years by natives of this country. These are not the general conditions, but they are the exceptions.

It is true that a very considerable portion of immigrants do not come to remain, but return after they have acquired some means, or because they find themselves unable to cope with the conditions of a new and aggressive country. Those who return for the latter reason relieve us of their own volition of a burden. Those who return after they have acquired some means certainly must be ad-

The Open Door Closes

In the first decade of the twentieth century, nearly 9 million people immigrated to the United States. Many Americans were feeling overwhelmed by the large number of immigrants and demanded that Congress do something to restrict immigration. In 1921, Congress set a quota limit for immigrants based on each country's immigrant population already in the United States according to the census of 1910. The quotas were modified three years later in the Immigration Act of 1924. Even though the act sharply reduced the number of immigrants entering the United States, Americans still questioned immigration policy. Herbert Block, a cartoonist for the Washington Post, *drew this political cartoon in 1946 as Americans continued to debate who should be allowed to immigrate to the United States.*

"What Happened To The One We Used To Have?"

The Herblock Book (Beacon Press, 1952). © 1952 by Herblock. Reprinted with permission.

mitted to have left with us a consideration for the advantage which they have enjoyed. A careful examination of the character of the people who come to stay and of the employment in which a large part of the new immigration is engaged will, in my judgment, dispel the apprehension which many of our people entertain.

The census will disclose that with rapid strides the foreign-born citizen is acquiring the farmlands of this county. Even if the foreign-born alone is considered, the percentage of his ownership is assuming a proportion that ought to attract the attention of the native citizens. If the second generation is included, it is safe to say that in the Middle West and West a majority of the farms are today owned by foreign-born people or they are descendants of the first generation. This does not embrace only the Germans and the Scandinavians but is true, in large measure, for illustration, of the Bohemians and the Poles. It is true in surprising measure of the Italians; not only of the northern Italians but of the southern.

We Get What We Need

Again, an examination of the aliens who come to stay is of great significance. During the last fiscal year, 838,172 aliens came to our shores, although the net immigration of the year was only a trifle above 400,000. But, while we received of skilled labor 127,016, and only 35,898 returned; we received servants, 116,529, and only 13,449 returned; we received farm laborers, 184,154, and only 3,978 returned, it appears that laborers came in the number of 135,726, while 209,279 returned. These figures ought to demonstrate that we get substantially what we most need and what we cannot ourselves supply, and that we get rid of what we least need and what seems to furnish, in the minds of many, the chief justification for the bill now under discussion.

The census returns show conclusively that the importance of illiteracy among aliens is overestimated and that these people are prompt after their arrival to avail of the opportunities which this country affords. While, according to the reports of the Bureau of Immigration, about 25 percent of the incoming aliens are illiterate, the census shows that among the foreign-born people of such states as New York and Massachusetts, where most of the congestion complained of has taken place, the proportion of illiteracy represents only about 13 percent.

I am persuaded that this provision of the bill is in principle of very great consequence, and that it is based upon a fallacy in undertaking to apply a test which is not calculated to reach the truth and to find relief from a danger which really does not exist. This provision of the bill is new, and it is radical. It goes to the heart of the measure. It does not permit of compromise, and, much as I regret it, because the other provisions of the measure are in most respects excellent and in no respect really objectionable, I am forced to advise that you do not approve this bill.

Viewpoint 4

"The exclusion of immigrants unable to read or write . . . will operate against the most undesirable and harmful part of our present immigration."

The Literacy Test Will Preserve America's Natural Superiority

Henry Cabot Lodge

Henry Cabot Lodge was a U.S. senator from Massachusetts and a member of the Immigration Restriction League, an anti-immigrant organization that was prominent from its founding in 1894 until the 1920s. In the following viewpoint, an excerpt from a speech he gave before the Senate in 1896 in support of a bill proposing a literacy test for immigrants, Lodge asserts that requiring a literacy test for new immigrants would weed out the worst of the new immigrants; those who passed the test would be able to assimilate more easily into American culture. Lodge claims that the values of the new immigrants, mostly from southern and eastern Europe, are incompatible with American ideals. In addition, the mixing of races through interracial marriage would pollute the white American race.

Henry Cabot Lodge, address to the U.S. Senate, March 16, 1896.

Mr. President, this bill is intended to amend the existing law so as to restrict still further immigration to the United States. Paupers, diseased persons, convicts, and contract laborers are now excluded. By this bill it is proposed to make a new class of excluded immigrants and add to those which have just been named the totally ignorant. The bill is of the simplest kind. The first section excludes from the country all immigrants who can not read and write either their own or some other language. The second section merely provides a simple test for determining whether the immigrant can read or write, and is added to the bill so as to define the duties of the immigrant inspectors, and to assure to all immigrants alike perfect justice and a fair test of their knowledge.

Two questions arise in connection with this bill. The first is as to the merits of this particular form of restriction; the second as to the general policy of restricting immigration at all. I desire to discuss briefly these two questions in the order in which I have stated them. The smaller question as to the merits of this particular bill comes first. The existing laws of the United States now exclude, as I have said, certain classes of immigrants who, it is universally agreed, would be most undesirable additions to our population. These exclusions have been enforced and the results have been beneficial, but the excluded classes are extremely limited and do not by any means cover all or even any considerable part of the immigrants whose presence here is undesirable or injurious, nor do they have any adequate effect in properly reducing the great body of immigration to this country. There can be no doubt that there is a very earnest desire on the part of the American people to restrict further and much more extensively than has yet been done foreign immigration to the United States. The question before the committee was how this could best be done; that is, by what method the largest number of undesirable immigrants and the smallest possible number of desirable immigrants could be shut out. Three methods of obtaining this further restriction have been widely discussed of late years and in various forms have been brought to the attention of Congress. The first was the imposition of a capitation tax on all immigrants. There can be no doubt as to the effectiveness of this method if the tax is made sufficiently heavy. But although exclusion by a tax would be thorough, it would be undiscriminating, and your committee did not feel that the time had yet come for its application. The second scheme was to restrict immigration by requiring consular certification of immigrants. This plan has been much advocated, and if it were possible to carry it out thoroughly and to add very largely to the number of our consuls in order to do so, it would no doubt be effective and beneficial. But the committee was satisfied that consular certification was, under existing circumstances, impractical; that the necessary machinery could not be provided; that it would lead to many serious questions with foreign governments, and that it could not be properly and justly enforced. . . .

Literacy Test Will Most Affect Undesirable Aliens

The third method was to exclude all immigrants who could neither read nor write, and this is the plan which was adopted by the committee and which is embodied in this bill. In their report the committee have shown by statistics, which have been collected and tabulated with great care, the emigrants who would be affected by this illiteracy test. It is not necessary for me here to do more than summarize the results of the committee's investigation, which have been set forth fully in their report. It is found, in the first place, that the illiteracy test will bear most heavily upon the Italians, Russians, Poles, Hungarians, Greeks, and Asiatics, and very lightly, or not at all, upon English-speaking emigrants or Germans, Scandinavians, and French. In other words, the races most affected by the illiteracy test are those whose emigration to this country has begun within the last twenty years and swelled rapidly to enormous proportions, races with which the English-speaking people have never hitherto assimilated, and who are most alien to the great body of the people of the United States. On the other hand, immigrants from the United Kingdom and of those races which are most closely related to the English-speaking people, and who with the English-speaking people themselves founded the American colonies and built up the United States, are affected but little by the proposed test. These races would not be prevented by this law from coming to this country in practically undiminished numbers. These kindred races also are those who alone go to the

Western and Southern States, where immigrants are desired, and take up our unoccupied lands. The races which would suffer most seriously by exclusion under the proposed bill furnish the immigrants who do not go to the West or South, where immigration is needed, but who remain on the Atlantic Seaboard, where immigration is not needed and where their presence is most injurious and undesirable.

Reduce City Congestion

The statistics prepared by the committee show further that the immigrants excluded by the illiteracy test are those who remain for the most part in congested masses in our great cities. They furnish, as other tables show, a large proportion of the population of the slums. The committee's report proves that illiteracy runs parallel with the slum population, with criminals, paupers, and juvenile delinquents of foreign birth or parentage, whose percentage is out of all proportion to their share of the total population when compared with the percentage of the same classes among the native born. It also appears from investigations which have been made that the immigrants who would be shut out by the illiteracy test are those who bring [the] least money to the country and come most quickly upon private or public charity for support. The replies of the governors of twenty-six States to the Immigration Restriction League show that in only two cases are immigrants of the classes affected by the illiteracy test desired, and those are of a single race. All the other immigrants mentioned by the governors as desirable belong to the races which are but slightly affected by the provisions of this bill. It is also proved that the classes now excluded by law, the criminals, the diseased, the paupers, and the contract laborers, are furnished chiefly by the same races as those most affected by the test of illiteracy. The same is true as to those immigrants who come to this country for a brief season and return to their native land, taking with them the money they have earned in the United States. There is no more hurtful and undesirable class of immigrants from every point of view than these "birds of passage," and the tables show that the races furnishing the largest number of "birds of passage" have also the greatest proportion of illiterates.

These facts prove to demonstration that the exclusion of immigrants unable to read or write, as proposed by this bill, will operate against the most undesirable and harmful part of our present immigration and shut out elements which no thoughtful or patriotic man can wish to see multiplied among the people of the United States. The report of the committee also proves that this bill meets the great requirement of all legislation of this character in excluding the greatest proportion possible of thoroughly undesirable and dangerous immigrants and the smallest proportion of immigrants who are unobjectionable.

I have said enough to show what the effects of this bill would be, and that if enacted into law it would be fair in its operation and highly beneficial in its results. It now remains for me to discuss the second and larger question, as to the advisability of restricting immigration at all. This is a subject of the greatest magnitude and the most far-reaching importance. It has two sides, the economic and the social. As to the former, but few words are necessary. There is no one thing which does so much to bring about a reduction of wages and to injure the American wage earner as the unlimited introduction of cheap foreign labor through unrestricted immigration. Statistics show that the change in the race character of our immigration has been accompanied by a corresponding decline in its quality. The number of skilled mechanics and of persons trained to some occupation or pursuit has fallen off, while the number of those without occupation or training, that is, who are totally unskilled, has risen in our recent immigration to enormous proportions. This low, unskilled labor is the most deadly enemy of the American wage earner, and does more than anything else toward lowering his wages and forcing down his standard of living. An attempt was made, with the general assent of both political parties, to meet this crying evil some years ago by the passage of what are known as the contract-labor laws. That legislation was excellent in intention, but has proved of but little value in practice. It has checked to a certain extent the introduction of cheap, low-class labor in large masses into the United States. It has made it a little more difficult for such labor to come here, but the labor of this class continues to come, even if not in the same way, and the total amount of it has not been materially reduced. Even if the contract-labor laws were enforced intelligently and thoroughly, there is no reason to suppose that they would have any adequate effect in checking the evil which they were designed to stop. It is perfectly clear after the experience of several years that the only relief which can come to the American wage earner from the competition of low-class immigrant labor must be by general laws restricting the total amount of immigration and framed in such a way as to affect most strongly those elements of the immigration which furnish the low, unskilled, and ignorant foreign labor.

It is not necessary to enter further into a discussion of the economic side of the general policy of restricting immigration. In this direction the argument is unanswerable. If we have any regard for the welfare, the wages, or the standard of life of American workingmen, we should take immediate steps to restrict foreign immigration. There is no danger, at present at all events, to our workingmen from the coming of skilled mechanics or of trained and educated men with a settled occupation or pursuit, for immigrants of this class will never seek to lower the American standard of life and wages. On the contrary, they desire the same standard for themselves. But there is an appalling danger to the American wage earner from the flood of low, unskilled, ignorant foreign labor which has poured into the country for some years past, and which not only takes lower wages, but accepts a standard of life and living so low that the American workingman can not compete with it.

Foreigners Harm the American Race

I now come to the aspect of this question which is graver and more serious than any other. The injury of unrestricted immigration to American wages and American standards of living is sufficiently plain and is bad enough, but the danger which this immigration threatens to the quality of our citizenship is far worse. That which it concerns us to know and that which is more vital to us as a people than all possible questions of tariff or currency is whether the quality of our citizenship is endangered by the present course and character of immigration to the United States. . . .

During the present century, down to 1875, there have been three large migrations to this country in addition to the always steady stream from Great Britain; one came from Ireland about the middle of the century, and somewhat later one from Germany and one from Scandinavia, in which is included Sweden, Denmark, and Norway. The Irish, although of a different race stock originally, have been closely associated with the English-speaking people for nearly a thousand years. They speak the same language, and during that long period the two races have lived side by side, and to some extent intermarried. The Germans and Scandinavians are again people of the same race stock as the English who founded and built up the colonies. During this century, down to 1875, then, as in the two which preceded it, there had been scarcely any immigration to this country, except from kindred or allied races, and no other, which was sufficiently numerous to have produced any effect on the national characteristics, or to be taken into account here. Since 1875, however, there has been a great change. While the people who for two hundred and fifty years have been migrating to America have continued to furnish large numbers of immigrants to the United States, other races of totally different race origin, with whom the English-speaking people have never hitherto been assimilated or brought in contact, have suddenly begun to immigrate to the United States in large numbers. Russians, Hungarians, Poles, Bohemians, Italians, Greeks, and even Asiatics, whose immigration to America was almost unknown twenty years ago, have during the last twenty years poured in in steadily increasing numbers, until now they nearly equal the immigration of those races kindred in blood or speech, or both, by whom the United States has hitherto been built up and the American people formed.

This momentous fact is the one which confronts us today, and if continued, it carries with it future consequences far deeper than any other event of our times. It involves, in a word, nothing less than the possibility of a great and perilous change in the very fabric of our race. The English-speaking race, as I have shown, has been made slowly during the centuries. Nothing has happened thus far to radically change it here. In the United States, after allowing for the variations produced by new climatic influences and changed conditions of life and of political institutions, it is still in the great essentials fundamentally the same race. The additions in this country until the present time have been from kindred people or from those with whom we have been long allied and who speak the same language. By those who look at this question superficially we hear it often said that the English-speaking people, especially in America, are a mixture of races. Analysis shows that the actual mixture of blood in the English-speaking race is very small, and that while the English-speaking people are derived through different channels, no doubt, there is among them none the less an overwhelming preponderance of the same race stock, that of the great Germanic tribes who reached from Norway to the Alps. They have been welded together by more than a thousand years of wars, conquests, migrations, and struggles, both at home and abroad, and in so doing they have attained a fixity and definiteness of national character unknown to any other people. . . .

When we speak of a race, then, we do not mean its expression in art or in language, or its achievements in knowledge. We mean the moral and intellectual characters, which in their association make the soul of a race, and which represent the product of all its past, the inheritance of all its ancestors, and the motives of all its conduct. The men of each race possess an indestructible stock of ideas, traditions, sentiments, modes of thought, an unconscious inheritance from their ancestors, upon which argument has no effect. What makes a race are their mental and, above all, their moral characteristics, the slow growth and accumulation of centuries of toil and conflict. These are the qualities which determine their social efficiency as a people, which make one race rise and another fall, which we draw out of a dim past through many generations of ancestors, about which we can not argue, but in which we blindly believe, and which guide us in our short-lived generation as they have guided the race itself across the centuries. . . .

Such achievements as M. Le Bon credits us with are due to the qualities of the American people, whom he, as a man of science looking below the surface, rightly describes as homogeneous. Those qualities are moral far more than intellectual, and it is on the moral qualities of the English-speaking race that our history, our victories, and all our future rest. There is only one way in which you can lower those qualities or weaken those characteristics, and that is by breeding them out. If a lower race mixes with a higher in sufficient numbers, history teaches us that the lower race will prevail. The lower race will absorb the higher, not the higher the lower, when the two strains approach equality in numbers. In other words, there is a limit to the capacity of any race to assimilating and elevating an inferior race, and when you begin to pour in in unlimited numbers people of alien or lower races of less social efficiency and less moral force, you are running the most frightful risk that any people can run. The lowering of a great race means not only its own decline but that of human civilization. M. Le Bon sees no danger to us in immigration, and his reason for this view is one of the most interesting things he says. He declares that the people of the United States will never be injured by immigration, because the moment they see the peril the great race instinct will assert itself and shut the immigration out. The reports of the Treasury for the last fifteen years show that the peril is at hand. I trust that the prediction of science is true and that the unerring instinct of the race will shut the danger out, as it closed the door upon the coming of the Chinese. . . .

Mr. President, more precious even than forms of government are the mental and moral qualities which make what we call our race. While those stand unimpaired all is safe. When those decline all is imperiled. They are exposed to but a single danger, and that is by changing the quality of our race and citizenship through the wholesale infusion of races whose traditions and inheritances, whose thoughts and whose beliefs are wholly alien to ours and with whom we have never assimilated or even been associated in the past. The danger has begun. It is small as yet, comparatively speaking, but it is large enough to warn us to act while there is yet time and while it can be done easily and efficiently. There lies the peril at the portals of our land; there is pressing in the tide of unrestricted immigration. The time has certainly come, if not to stop, at least to check, to sift, and to restrict those immigrants. In careless strength, with generous hand, we have kept our gates wide open to all the world. If we do not close them, we should at least place sentinels beside them to challenge those who would pass through. The gates which admit men to the United States and to citizenship in the great Republic should no longer be left unguarded.

Viewpoint 5

"Public opinion in America has upheld a policy of increasing [immigration] restriction."

Quota Acts Carry Out the Will of the American People

Roy L. Garis

In 1921 Congress passed the Emergency Quota Act, which for the first time placed a limit on the number of immigrants allowed into the United States. There were two main provisions of the 1921 law. First, it permitted a total of 350,000 immigrants to enter the United States per year. A second provision of the act limited the number of immigrants from a particular country to 3 percent of that country's population already in the United States as determined by the 1910 census. For example, the 1921 quota act permitted forty-two thousand Italians and thirty-one thousand Poles to immigrate to the United States. When the 1921 quota act came up for renewal in 1924, anti-immigrationists made the act even more restrictive. The Immigration Act of 1924 reduced the percentage allowed from each country to 2 percent of the nationality's population in the United States (thus lowering the total number allowed to immigrate to approximately three hundred thousand), and changed the baseline census from 1910—which included many eastern and southern Europeans—

Roy L. Garis, *North American Review*, 1924.

to 1890, when very few eastern and southern Europeans lived in the United States. Thus, under the 1924 quota act, the Italian quota was reduced to four thousand immigrants and the Polish quota cut to six thousand.

In the following viewpoint, Roy L. Garis contends that the 1924 quota act reducing the number and composition of the immigrants is necessary. America was primarily founded by immigrants from Great Britain, Ireland, Germany, and Scandinavia; these people have similar blood, political ideals, and economic and social backgrounds. Assimilation was fast and easy for these immigrants. The "new" immigrants, Garis maintains, are from completely different stock—the Mediterranean and Slavic countries of Russia, Austria-Hungary, Italy, and Turkey. Not only are they of different races but also of different religions and cultures. Their people are illiterate, primitive, and inferior in every way to the "old" and desirable immigrants from northern and western Europe, he asserts. Reducing the number of "new" immigrants will give Americans time to educate and assimilate them while still allowing the "old" immigrants—who assimilate easily—to come.

Garis was an economist at Vanderbilt University and the author of several books and articles about immigration, including *Immigration Restriction: A Study of the Opposition to and Regulation of Immigration into the United States.*

The important provisions of the Immigration Act of 1924, signed by President [Calvin] Coolidge on May 26, are: (1) it preserves the basic immigration law of 1917; (2) it retains the principle of numerical limitation as inaugurated in the act of May 19, 1921; (3) it changes the quota basis from the census of 1910 to the census of 1890; (4) it reduces the quota admissible in any one year from 3 to 2 per cent.; (5) it provides a method of selection of immigrants at the source rather than to permit them to come to this country and land at the immigration stations without previous inspection; (6) it reduces the classes of exempted aliens; (7) it places the burden of proof on the alien to show that he is admissible under the immigration laws rather than upon the United

States to show that he is not admissible; and (8) it provides entire and absolute exclusion of those who are not eligible to become naturalized citizens under our naturalization laws.

While it was evident from the beginning that no law would please all, yet it is safe to say that at least eighty per cent. of the American people approve of the new provisions in the Act of 1924. The sources of opposition were and still are:

(1) Those who believe that the law is not sufficiently restrictive. For the most part this opposition was not a stumbling block.

(2) Those who believe that the law does not admit enough common laborers to do the rough work of the United States.

(3) Those who, while pretending to favor restriction, really want anybody and everybody except the insane, the criminal and the diseased, so that they may proceed to reap dividends from their particular lines of endeavor, whether the lines be mills, factories, steamships, newspapers of various languages, or the like, in addition to bondsmen, some lawyers, common crooks, and others who daily exploit the newly arrived alien.

(4) Those of an international mind, who think that migrations should not be impeded, except possibly from China, Korea, Japan and India.

(5) Those who for religious, racial, or family reasons desire more of their own to be residents of the United States.

(6) Those who have been led to believe that the United States can go throughout the world handpicking bricklayers here, plasterers there, gardeners elsewhere and farmers at another place, and bring them, without thought of families, to our States; in other words, selection, distribution and supervision. . . .

Selfish Altruism

A great deal of cant and hypocrisy is being preached at the present day as to the motives that lie back of the attitude of the American Government and the American people toward immigration of the past. "A political asylum," "a haven of refuge," "a welcome to the oppressed," "a home for the persecuted"—these and like phrases are all fine, high-sounding expressions, and we believe in them as did our forefathers. But the fact is, they express a secondary and not the primary cause underlying the action of our people and Government toward the alien.

This primary basis has always been what might be called selfish altruism. We have welcomed the immigrant, not because he was an alien, not because he was escaping religious or political persecution, not because he was down-trodden and oppressed, but primarily and essentially because we believed his coming here was for our own good as a people and as a nation. We have welcomed him only so long as, and no longer than, we believed this. When we had been made to realize that his arrival was dangerous and fraught with injury to us, we objected to his coming and took steps to prevent it—even from colonial times. And once having taken a step forward—once having put up a bar—we have never let it down again or taken a step backward. . . .

American People Oppose Immigration

It [is] evident that from colonial times the American people have opposed the coming of immigrants into this country when they had to associate with them and enter into competition with them; that so long as there was plenty of land—a frontier—and the immigrants were willing to go to it, the problem was not acute; that the young Republic was forced in self-defense to pass drastic laws against the aliens; that with the passing of the years in the last century the opposition to immigrants became more and more crystallized and found expression in one restrictive measure after another until prior to the Act of 1924 less than 400,000 immigrants could enter the United States in any fiscal year under the 3 per cent. law; and lastly but most important of all, that once having passed a restrictive measure, the American people have never repealed it, but have expressed themselves time and time again to be in favor of more severe measures of restriction.

If America can be said to have had a traditional immigration policy, it has certainly not been one upholding free and unrestrictive immigration. On the other hand public opinion in America has upheld a policy of increasing restriction and this, if anything, has been her traditional policy. The American people want restriction, strict, severe restriction. The bars must be put up higher and more scientifically. Practical results are demanded. Does the Act of 1924 take steps in this direction? Does it grant what the public wants in concrete terms?

In the first place and without question, the American people wanted the Act of 1917 excluding certain classes to be continued and strengthened—the most important of these classes being idiots, imbeciles, feeble-minded persons, epileptics, insane persons, paupers, beggars, vagrants, persons afflicted with disease, criminals, polygamists, anarchists, persons likely to become a public charge, illiterates, etc. Such persons as these must be excluded even though they might be eligible for admittance under every other provision of the law. The Act of 1924 continues and strengthens the exclusion of such classes.

Public Opinion and the "New" Immigrants

In the second place and beyond doubt, public opinion is opposed to the so-called "new" immigration and desired its restriction to the lowest possible minimum.

At the present time European immigration to the United States may be divided into two groups, the "old" and the "new." The "old" immigration extended from the beginning of our national history to about the year 1890 and was derived chiefly from Great Britain and Ireland, Germany, and the Scandinavian countries. Thus practically all the immigrants to 1890 were predominantly Anglo-Saxon-Germanic in blood and Protestant in religion—of the same stock as that which originally settled the United States, wrote our Constitution and established our democratic institutions. The English, Dutch, Swedes, Germans, and even the Scotch-Irish, who constituted practically the entire immigration, were less than two thousand years ago one Germanic race in the forests surrounding the North Sea. Thus being similar in blood and in political ideals, social training, and economic background, this "old" immigration merged with the native stock fairly easily and rapidly. Assimilation was only a matter of time and this was aided by the economic, social and political conditions of the country. Even though those who were already here objected to others coming in, yet once in they soon became Americans, so assimilated as to be indistinguishable from the natives. Furthermore, in comparison with the present-day immigration it was relatively small in volume, while the abundance of free land and our need for pioneers prevented the rise of any serious problem.

In the period centering about the year 1880, and in particular in the decade 1880–1890, there was a distinct shift in the immigration movement. Whereas before 1890 most of our immigrants had been Anglo-Saxons and Teutons from Northern Europe, after 1890 the majority were members of the Mediterranean and Slavic races from Southern and Southeastern Europe. The great bulk of this "new" immigration has its source in Russia, Poland, Austria, Hungary, Greece, Turkey, Italy and the Balkan countries. It is in connection with this "new" immigration that the present immigration problem exists. Its solution challenges our attention.

Separating the Desirable from the Undesirable

As Professor Commons says: "A line drawn across the continent of Europe from northeast to southwest, separating the Scandinavian Peninsula, the British Isles, Germany, and France from Russia, Austria-Hungary, Italy, and Turkey, separates countries not only of distinct races but also of distinct civilizations. It separates Protestant Europe from Catholic Europe; it separates countries of representative institutions and popular government from monarchies; it separates lands where education is universal from lands where illiteracy predominates; it separates manufacturing countries, progressive agriculture, and skilled labor from primitive hand industries, backward agriculture, and unskilled labor; it separates an educated, thrifty peasantry from a peasantry scarcely a single generation removed from serfdom; it separates Teutonic races from Latin, Slav, Semitic, and Mongolian races. When the sources of American immigration are shifted from the Western countries so nearly allied to our own, to Eastern countries so remote in the main attributes of Western civilization, the change is one that should challenge the attention of every citizen."

The racial proportions of incoming aliens having thus undergone a remarkable change since 1890, the result has been "a swift and ominous lowering of the general average of character, intelligence, and moral stamina," with the result now that the situation is "full of menace and danger to our native racial stream and to our long-established institutions." The advocates of free and unre-

stricted immigration refute such a contention by pointing out that
the same has been said time and time again for over a hundred
years. They point to members of the old immigration and say that
all that these needed was an opportunity. They go to great trouble
to compare the present "new" immigration with the types which
came to us prior to 1890, in order to establish their contention that
the present "new" immigration is no worse than the former. However, I desire to point out in this connection a thought which I have
not found expressed in the arguments answering the above con-
tentions of the advocates of free immigration. It is simply this—
that the comparison of the present "new" immigration with the
lower types which came to us prior to 1890 is wasted energy. The
vital thing for us today is not whether the present "new" immigration is equal to, superior to, or lower than the immigration of
35 years ago, but how does it compare with the "old" immigration
of *today?* According to every test made in recent years and from a
practical study of the problem, it is evident beyond doubt that the
immigrant from Northern and Western Europe is far superior to
the one from Southern and Eastern Europe.

In the Act of 1924 Congress adopted a suggestion of the writer
that a simple and practical solution of the problems created by the
"new" immigration—a solution based on scientific and historical
facts—would be to adopt the census of 1890 instead of 1910 or
1920 as the basis for permanent legislation and future percentage
laws. It is true that the 3 per cent. law based on the census of 1910
was primarily quantitative, but it was nevertheless qualitative to
the extent that it kept from our shores millions of undesirables
which this country could afford to do without. The 2 per cent. law
based on the census of 1890 limits qualitatively to a much higher
degree as well as numerically within safe boundaries. It closes the
doors to all but a few thousand "new" immigrants each year. It
will give us time to educate and assimilate those now here (a task
of gigantic proportions, requiring many years). And yet such a
plan does not exclude to a detrimental point those immigrants
from Northern and Western Europe who might desire to come
and who are easily assimilated. Such a provision is eminently fair
and equitable, and yet it raised a storm of protest among the nationals whose quotas it reduced. But this is the invariable effect of

any legislative proposals that are frankly framed for the benefit of America and Americans rather than for Europe and Europeans. And yet, as in the case of any bill, the character of the opposition may be the strongest kind of evidence of intrinsic merit.

There are many industries in this country which are dependent upon foreign labor if wage scales and working hours of past years are to prevail. Native American labor will not work twelve-hour shifts when eight-hour jobs can be had. Americans will not be satisfied with the living conditions or the fare that the foreign-born laborer is satisfied with.

The solution of the labor shortage in these industries is either a revised schedule of employment or a free entry of labor from foreign countries. Yet to open the gates again to the common labor of foreign lands would be to surrender much of what we have gained. It would but add to our domestic problems, since the great majority of this class are unfitted for citizenship.

Some industries have not kept pace with other American industries either in working hours or wages. A labor shortage in such industries will probably be a direct result of this condition. The thinking man comes to regard such industries as a place to seek employment only when all other places fail, and to be left as soon as a job can be obtained elsewhere. A revision of standards in some of our industries is what is needed right now. Happily some have seen the handwriting on the wall and are taking such a step. American industries can get all the labor they need if they will give labor a square deal and cease treating it as a commodity.

Cater to Employers No More

Indeed, the time is opportune for Americans to insist on an American policy, regardless of what our employers of cheap labor and our foreign born want. We have catered to them too long already and in consequence have been throwing away our birthright. The vital thing is to preserve the American race, as far as it can be preserved, and build it up with Nordic stock; intelligent, literate, easily assimilated, appreciating and able to carry on our American institutions. The percentage law based on the census of 1890 will in time automatically bring about such a result.

In a recent letter to me, the Hon. Roger W. Babson stated: "Of course I am in favor of an extension of our Immigration Service to the points of embarkation on the other side." Perhaps no other provision in the Act of 1924 has met with such general approval as the one which provides for a form of examination over seas. For several years it seemed impossible to work out a practical method and one satisfactory to the nations in whose ports such inspection takes place. Under the new law both non-quota and quota immigrants are required to file their written application under oath in duplicate before the United States consul in their country for an immigration certificate. These applications go fully into their past records, their family history, and into their mental, moral and physical qualifications. This process now enables us to weed out in advance those not qualified for entrance into the United States. A satisfactory examination there procures an immigrant certificate for admission here, provided that the quota has not been exhausted. However, the certificate does not exempt the immigrant from a final inspection and medical examination at the port of entry. The immigrant is subject to deportation if he or she fails to measure up to the Act of 1917.

The law provides that not more than 10 per cent. of the total number of certificates allotted to each country may be issued in any one month, and a certificate is void four months after the date of issuance. The counting of these certificates is made abroad. A no more constructive provision could be imagined than this, for it eliminates the racing of steamships into the ports of entry on the first day of each month, it eliminates the necessity of immigrants being forced to return to Europe due to exhausted quotas, and at the same time it gives our consuls the power to prevent obviously undesirable aliens from coming to America.

The provision in the law abrogating the gentlemen's agreement with Japan, and excluding all Japanese laborers from the United States because of their ineligibility for citizenship, has been the subject of world discussion. Under this gentlemen's agreement Japan, not the United States, determined what and how many Japanese laborers could come to America. It was inevitable that this arrangement should be ended and Congress was within its rights in ending it, although it might have accomplished it in a more diplomatic manner.

It has been my purpose to explain briefly those provisions of the new law which have been subject to the most discussion in order to make clear that each provision is but a logical step forward in our traditional policy of increasing restriction of immigration in a more humane, scientific and constructive manner. The Secretary of Labor, Mr. Davis, said in a recent address, "There should be some immigration of the right kind, but we, not Europe, will say who shall come or we will not let any come." Certainly in the Act of 1924 we have taken important steps forward in the right direction toward permanent legislation worthy of the name.

Viewpoint 6

"Those who have come from the countries sought to be tabooed have been industrious and law-abiding and have made valuable contributions to our industrial, commercial and social development."

Quota Acts Are Unjust

Louis Marshall

In an attempt to restrict immigration from southern and eastern Europe, Congress passed the Emergency Quota Act of 1921. However, many anti-immigrationists believed that the act was ineffective at limiting the number of "undesirable" immigrants from Italy, Poland, and Russia, among others, and so Congress once again began examining ways to restrict these immigrants. A bill proposed in 1924 limited new immigration from a given country to 2 percent of that country's immigrant population in the United States in 1890, a date that was chosen because there were few immigrants from southern and eastern Europe in the United States at that time. The bill would also completely prohibit immigration from Japan, which had been strictly limited under an informal treaty known as the Gentlemen's Agreement.

The following viewpoint is an excerpt of a letter written on May 22, 1924, by Louis Marshall, a constitutional lawyer, and chairman and founder of the Jewish Relief Committee, to President Calvin Coolidge, who was deciding whether to sign the bill. (Coolidge did sign the bill into law on May 26.) Marshall argues that excluding all Japanese immigrants—who were previously limited to about 250 immigrants per year—is insulting and of-

Louis Marshall, letter to Calvin Coolidge, May 22, 1924.

fensive to a nation that is considered America's political equal. He then goes on to the main point of his argument: The bill discriminates against southern and eastern Europeans who are believed to be "inferior" to the "preferred" northern and western Europeans. There is absolutely no basis for this belief, he contends; southern and eastern European immigrants are law-abiding and hardworking citizens whose children are educated and Americanized in public schools. These immigrants have assimilated into American culture readily and well, and to discriminate against them stimulates racial hatred. Furthermore, basing the limits on national origins completely ignores the prospective immigrants' usefulness to the United States.

O n behalf of many hundred thousands of citizens of the United States, both native-born and naturalized, who feel slighted by the terms of the Immigration Bill now before you for Executive action, and availing ourselves of your permission, we venture to state reasons justifying your disapproval of the measure.

A Deep Insult to Japan

Before proceeding to a consideration of the main objections urged by those for whom we speak, it is fitting to refer, as symptomatic of the atmosphere of racial hostility which permeates this proposed legislation, to the provision which is intended to terminate forthwith the so-called Gentlemen's Agreement with the Empire of Japan and to exclude from the quota privileges conferred by the act all subjects of that Government. At the Disarmament Conference there was complete cooperation, and the desire on the part of Japan for maintaining amicable relations toward us has been consistently sincere. Past experience demonstrates that, however distasteful to Japan discriminatory legislation on the subject of immigration may be, there can be no doubt that, by means of appropriate diplomatic procedure, which would avoid the placing of an affront upon a proud people, a satisfactory arrangement regarding immigration, based on mutual consent, can be arrived at between the two countries.

Instead of permitting such an obviously conciliatory method to be pursued by the treaty-making branch of our Government, this bill, in the most offensive manner and in total disregard of the natural feelings of a sister nation, whom we have regarded as a political equal, inflicts a deep insult upon the national and racial consciousness of a highly civilized and progressive country. Such a wound will never cease to rankle. It will give rise to hostility which, even when not apparent on the surface, will prove most serious. It cannot fail to be reflected upon our commerce, and in days of stress will be likely to occasion unspeakable concern. And what will be the net result upon immigration by the elimination of Japan from the quota provisions? The exclusion of possibly 250 immigrants a year at a time when a large number of Japanese now in this country are emigrating annually.

The Quota Law

Coming now to the principal purpose of this communication:

(1) The central provision of this bill is that contained in Section 11, subdivision (a), which limits the annual quota of any nationality to two per centum of the number of foreign-born individuals of such nationality residing in continental United States as determined by the census of 1890, the minimum quota to any nationality being 100.

The present quota law is based on the census of 1910 and fixes a rate of three per cent. That idea was fathered by the late Senator [William P.] Dillingham, who had given the subject careful study as the Chairman of the Immigration Commission appointed during President [Theodore] Roosevelt's Administration. He proposed a rate of five per cent., but it was reduced while the bill was on its passage. The census of 1910 was chosen because that of 1920 was not then available. The idea was that the proper test was the number of foreign-born individuals of the various nationalities in the country at the time the quota was to become effective. Even that bill gave rise to great hardships. It was, however, fair, in that it did not discriminate among the foreign-born individuals of various nationalities.

A Discriminatory Bill

The present bill, however, is avowedly discriminatory, as is apparent from the Majority and Minority Reports of the House Committee on Immigration which reported this bill. While under the present law the number of immigrants who come from Northern and Western Europe and of those who come from Southern and Eastern Europe are equal, under this bill the number of immigrants who may come from Northern and Western Europe is largely increased, even on the reduced basis of two per cent., over the number admitted from those countries under the present law; whereas those coming from Southern and Eastern Europe will not exceed one-fifth of those now admitted from that portion of Europe. . . .

This is the first time in the history of American legislation that there has been an attempt to discriminate in respect to European immigration between those who come from different parts of the continent. It is not only a differentiation as to countries of origin, but also of racial stocks and of religious beliefs. Those coming from Northern and Western Europe are supposed to be Anglo-Saxon or mythical Nordics, and to a large extent Protestant. Those coming from Southern and Eastern Europe are of different racial stocks and of a different faith. There are today in this country millions of citizens, both native-born and naturalized, descended from those racial stocks and entertaining those religious beliefs against which this bill deliberately discriminates. There is no mincing of the matter.

No Justification

To add insult to injury, the effort has been made to justify this class legislation by charging that those who are sought to be excluded are inferior types and not assimilable. There is no justification in fact for such a contention. In common with all other immigrants, those who have come from the countries sought to be tabooed have been industrious and law-abiding and have made valuable contributions to our industrial, commercial and social development. They have done the hard, manual work which is indispensable to normal economic growth. Their children, educated in our public schools, are as American in their outlook as are those of the immigrants of earlier periods. Some of the intellectual leaders of the nation have sprung from this decried origin. During the World War [I] some of these very immigrants and their children fought for the country, thousands of them waiving the exemption to which they would have been entitled.

To say that they are not assimilable argues ignorance. The facts show that they adopt American standards of living and that they are permeated with the spirit of our institutions. It is said that they speak foreign languages, but in those foreign languages they are taught to love our Government, and to a very great extent they are acquiring the use of the English language as completely as most Americans would acquire foreign languages were they to migrate to other countries.

Under the existing basic Immigration Act of 1917, which is a highly selective law, ample provision is made for the exclusion of those who are mentally, morally and physically unfit, of those who are likely to become public charges, and of those who entertain views which are opposed to organized government and not consonant with our institutions. It has been the boast of those who have advocated the legislation now under consideration, that the United States has ceased to be an asylum of the oppressed; and one of the projectors of this bill has declared it to be a new Declaration of Independence, forgetting that the old Declaration, in reciting the injuries and usurpations of the British monarch, charged: "He has endeavored to prevent the population of these States, for that purpose obstructing the laws for naturalization of foreigners; refusing to pass others to encourage their migrations hither, and raising the conditions of new appropriations of lands." Let us not forget that what has made ours a noble nation has been the fact that we have received the oppressed and have admitted to our shores men and women who were worthy of sharing the opportunities afforded by our tremendous national resources, which, to an extraordinary extent, still clamor for development.

What we regard as the danger lurking in this legislation is, that it stimulates racial, national and religious hatreds and jealousies, that it encourages one part of our population to arrogate to itself a sense of superiority, and to classify another as one of inferiority. At a time when the welfare of the human race as an entirety depends upon the creation of a brotherly spirit, the restoration of peace, harmony and unity, and the termination of past animosities engendered by the insanity and brutality of war, it should be our purpose, as a nation which has demonstrated that those of diverse racial, national and religious origins can live together and prosper as a united people, to serve as the world's conciliator. Instead of that this bill, if it becomes a law, is destined to become the very Apple of Discord.

An Attempt to Limit Immigration

(2) Subdivision (b) of Section 11 only adds to the injustice and the confusion of thought which characterize this bill. Instead of dealing with what was claimed by the Dillingham bill to be an emergency and leaving it to future Congresses to take up the subject anew, this section provides that the annual quota of any nationality for the fiscal year beginning July 1, 1927, *and for each fiscal year thereafter*, shall be a number which bears the same ratio to 150,000 as the number of immigrants in continental United States in 1920 having that national origin bears to the number of inhabitants in continental United States in 1920. This attempts to fix indefinitely, beginning three years hence, the number of immigrants to be admitted at 150,000.

Heretofore we have had no difficulty in absorbing a million immigrants a year. From August, 1914, down to 1920, because of the war, there were practically no immigrants into the United States—in fact during that period the emigrants exceeded in number the immigrants; and yet there is an attempt to determine once [and] for all the number of immigrants who are to be admitted into our vast domain to supply our industries and to meet our many other needs.

But here, again, the vice of the legislation is that it is based entirely on national origin, regardless of fitness or usefulness, diligence or energy, or of our country's needs. Moreover, the reference to "national origin" is not to the number of foreign-born individuals of the several nationalities resident in the United States, but it is expected to make a biological, anthropological, ethnological investigation into the birth or ancestry of those resident in the United States in 1920. It is believed that there are no statistics which would make it possible to work out a reliable conclusion as to national origin. The very fact that there have been intermarriages between those of diverse nationalities and that there may be an admixture of the blood of half a dozen nationalities into a single individual, demonstrates the absurdity of such a scheme. There has been no scientific or other investigation indicating that it is practicable to work out such a theory, and yet it is written into our law as a happy thought originating during the heat of argument.

It is evident that three years will be required to make the determination called for, and yet, in advance of any trustworthy investigation, the fundamental theory of our immigration laws, in force for more than a century and by means of which we have progressed as no other nation in the world has during a like period, is to be forever rejected. It will be a sorry day for our Republic when our national legislation shall substitute for the humane, farsighted and statesmanlike theories of the past, the feudal, medieval and inhuman concepts which characterize this bill.

Separating Families

(3) Although it has been the declared public policy of this country not to separate families, under the present bill, with its reduced quotas, where practically every immigrant is to be governed by the quota principle, it will become virtually impossible for a wife and children of a husband and father coming to this country for the purpose of establishing a home for them to join the head of the household. The fact that under Section 6 (a) they are entitled to preference will be of but little avail in the light of the diminished quotas. Nor does Section 4, subdivision (a), remedy the situation, because it deals merely with the unmarried child under the age of 18 years, or the wife, of a citizen of the United States. In such cases a period of five years may elapse during which the separation would be continued.

Non-Quota Immigrants

(4) Further discrimination is shown by the fact that under Section 4 (c) an immigrant born in the Dominion of Canada, Newfoundland, the Republic of Mexico, the Republic of Cuba, the Republic of Haiti, the Dominican Republic, the Canal Zone, or an independent country of Central or South America, and his wife and his unmarried children under eighteen years of age, are admitted as non-quota immigrants. Can it be seriously contended that Mexicans, Cubans, Haitians, Santo Domingoans, or Central or South Americans, are more desirable or more assimilable than

Italians, Poles, Russians, Austrians, Belgians, Hungarians, Roumanians, Greeks, Dutch, Czechoslovakians or Yugoslavians?

The Burden of Proof

(5) Section 24 reverses the rule of evidence which has always hitherto obtained, by seeking to impose the burden of proof upon the alien to establish that he is not subject to exclusion under any provision of the immigration law, and that in any deportation proceeding against any alien the burden of proof shall be upon him to show that he entered the United States lawfully. By the operation of this provision, if an immigrant arrives here and is told that the quota of his nationality had on the day previous been exhausted, it will be necessary for him to prove the contrary, although the records are within the control of the Government and it is utterly impossible for the immigrant to establish by legal evidence the inaccuracy of the statement that he was not admissible.

You will recollect, Mr. President, that in the early part of November, 1923, it was announced by the Department of Labor that the Russian quota for the year had been exhausted, and approximately 1,000 immigrants were excluded and ordered deported. Some of the cases were of excruciating hardship. Two hundred of them were in fact deported, when it was learned that, through erroneous bookkeeping in the Department or otherwise, all of these arrivals were admissible. The facts being called to your attention, those remaining in this country were promptly admitted. Let us suppose that the burden of proof to show that they were entitled to admission rested on these immigrants. It would not have been possible to have met it. If habeas corpus proceedings had been instituted the Government would have stood mute and the writ would necessarily have been dismissed.

Illustrations could be multiplied to show that such a rule of evidence as is now contemplated is not only unjust and inequitable, but contrary to American traditions.

Without dwelling upon other objections, we most respectfully and earnestly submit that if this bill shall become a law it will be a positive misfortune to the country and will mark a sharp departure from those policies which have proven a blessing to mankind as well as to our beloved land.

Viewpoint 7

"For the first time in American history, immigration into the United States was denied on the basis of race and class. Chinese now joined the ranks of imbeciles, paupers, prostitutes, and felons as official 'undesirables.'"

The Chinese Exclusion Act Was Discriminatory

Jennie F. Lew

The following viewpoint is an excerpt from a 1994 television program titled *Separate Lives, Broken Dreams: Saga of Chinese Immigration*, produced by Jennie F. Lew.

During the mid-1850s, China was experiencing a depression caused by years of drought, then floods, disease, and famine. At the same time, California was in the midst of its gold rush. The lure of riches proved to be irresistible to thousands of Chinese, who left their homes in search of a better life. Although initially welcomed as a dependable and inexpensive workforce, the Chinese were eventually blamed for the lowered wages, unemployment, and poor working conditions of the American depression that followed in the 1870s. Americans unleashed their prejudices against the Chinese, claiming they did not assimilate into

Jennie F. Lew, "Separate Lives, Broken Dreams: Saga of Chinese Immigration," www.naatanet.org, 2002. Copyright © 2002 by National Asian American Telecommunications Association & Jennie Lew. Reproduced by permission.

American society. Eventually, laws and local ordinances against Chinese workers were passed; these ranged from petty harassment to laws that threatened the livelihood and civil rights of the Chinese. These laws culminated in the Chinese Exclusion Act of 1882, which suspended the immigration of Chinese workers to the United States for ten years. Lew notes that the Chinese Exclusion Act was the first time that a specific group had been singled out and denied permission to immigrate to the United States because of race and class. The Chinese considered the law unjust and discriminatory. According to Lew, many Chinese tried to get around the exclusions by different means, such as smuggling themselves in or buying false identity papers.

The Chinese Exclusion Act was extended to include other Asians—Japanese, Koreans, Filipinos, and Asian Indians. The act was not repealed until 1943. And because of the severe restrictions imposed on the Chinese during this period, there were very few Chinese immigrants in the United States to be counted in the 1890 census, which was the basis of the Immigration Act of 1924 that limited incoming immigrants to a quota of 2 percent of their immigrant numbers in 1890. Ethnic restrictions were not abolished until 1965.

Beginning in the mid-19th century, Chinese immigration to America was influenced by both the "pull" of California's Gold Rush and the "push" created by China's impoverished conditions. Years of drought, floods, disease, and famine ravaged China, a country already burdened with overpopulation and internal instability. European and American exploits into the region further exacerbated China's economic, political, and social problems.

The Gold Mountain

Chinese peasants, particularly in the rural Pearl River Delta area in the southeastern province of Guangdong, were desperate for relief. They began to migrate to urban centers in search of employment and survival. When this proved insufficient, the Chinese migrated to Southeast Asia and the Pacific Region (e.g., Thailand, Singapore, Malaysia, Indonesia, and the Philippines). Word soon reached China that "Gum Saan," the "Gold Mountain" as the Chinese referred to America, was a land of opportunity for those seeking a better life.

The first large number of Chinese arriving in America in the mid-1850s, like many other immigrants to the new land, found no "gold mountain" from which instant wealth could be attained. However, America's expansion to the West and the economic boom of the Gold Rush era did provide particular employment possibilities for the Chinese. They quickly became an inexpensive but formidable work force for the construction of the western portion of the transcontinental rail system. They also played an important role in the development of the agricultural, fishing, and even manufacturing industries of the Western States.

By the early 1870s, the Gold Rush "boom" had turned into a "bust." Tens of thousands of East Coast laborers, traveling westward on the very railroad system built by the Chinese, faced an economy in decline and fierce competition for jobs. The Chinese, once welcomed for their work ethic and valuable contribution to the work force, were now blamed for lowering wages, employment opportunities, and working conditions of all laborers.

Long-held racial, cultural, and religious prejudices were unleashed on the so-called "heathen Chinese." Inclined to maintain the customs, rituals, beliefs, and lifestyle of their homeland, the Chinese were accused of being unable or unwilling to assimilate into American society. Public sentiment and organized labor began to advocate for restrictions on the activities of Chinese and changes in the immigration laws. In response, politicians eventually passed over 600 ordinances and laws against Asians throughout the United States. They ranged from local ordinances intent on petty harassment, to extremely mean-spirited and harmful state laws aimed at the very livelihood and civil rights of Chinese in America. Anti-Chinese sentiment escalated into violence, whereby Chinese residents and laborers were forcibly evicted from towns and work camps. In some cases, the Chinese were attacked and killed.

However, the Chinese community in America did not tolerate discrimination and abuse without protest. They organized and raised funds to hire expert legal representation to challenge the system in local, state, and Supreme Courts. Far from being passive victims, the Chinese in America won many precedent-setting cases, and in some instances, even reparations for damages. As local ordinances and state laws failed to curtail the activities and immigration of the Chinese, the move to restrict and exclude Chinese immigrants moved to a national platform.

The Chinese Exclusion Act was finally passed by Congress in 1880, and signed into law by President [Chester] Arthur on May 5, 1882. It suspended the immigration of Chinese laborers for ten years. In 1892, and again in 1902, it was extended for additional ten-year periods each. In 1904, the act was amended to run perpetually. For the first time in American history, immigration into the United States was denied on the basis of race and class. Chinese now joined the ranks of imbeciles, paupers, prostitutes, and felons as official "undesirables."

To maintain important trade relations with China, select classifications of Chinese were still permitted to enter the United States. Specifically, the Chinese allowed into the United States were travelers, merchants, diplomats (including their families and servants), students, and teachers. Numerous amendments later attempted to clarify certain provisions, close loopholes, and strengthen the overall restrictions introduced by the Act. Though subsequent legislation provided for the entry of the wives and families of Chinese merchants, it was clear that new Chinese immigrants of the laboring class and their family members would no longer be allowed in the United States.

Life Under Chinese Exclusion

All Chinese immigrants entering the country were now scrutinized under the severe restrictions of the Chinese Exclusion Act. The Port of San Francisco received the greatest number of Chinese. In the beginning, the Chinese were detained in a two-story, wooden warehouse operated by the Pacific Mail Steamship Company (an overseas transportation firm). Located on the San Francisco waterfront, this makeshift detention "shed" was considered an overcrowded "fire trap." Reports of lax security and improper ventilation and sanitation led to the construction of new detention facilities on Angel Island.

Though fraught with many of the same inadequacies, Angel Island Immigration Station eventually received tens of thousands of Chinese during the Exclusion period from 1910 to 1940. Entering Europeans, Japanese "picture brides" (destined to marry their prospective husbands by proxy in America), and other immigrants not subject to Chinese Exclusion were allowed to either land immediately in San Francisco, or experience short stays on Angel Island to confirm their status. On the other hand, U.S. immigration officials detained Chinese for extensive interrogations for several weeks, even months, and occasionally, a year or more.

The Chinese considered American Exclusion grossly unjust and discriminatory. Boycotts of American goods were organized in large Chinese communities as far away as the Philippines. Chinese diplomats in Hong Kong and community organizations in America would submit letters complaining about degrading practices and mistreatment by immigration officials. Many Chinese laborers and their family members resorted to methods for circumventing the Act. They would smuggle themselves across the border or purchase identity documents falsely claiming to be an individual of an exempt classification (e.g., a merchant or child of a merchant, or a U.S. citizen or child of a U.S. citizen). The creation of "border patrols," and indeed, the evolution of some of America's largest bureaucracies (the U.S. Customs Department, and Immigration and Naturalization Service, i.e., the I.N.S.) directly stems from much of the enforcement practices required by Chinese Exclusion.

Desperate attempts to enter America under Exclusion often involved the cooperation and assistance of different members of the Chinese community, as well as those in the white community. Chinese community organizations and import/export companies provided transportation, housing, exchange of important correspondence, and other means of support. Friendly members of the white community would sometimes bear both true and sometimes false "witness" to a person's residency or status as a merchant. Corrupt immigration officers could be involved in bribery schemes whereby false birth certificates would be issued or testimony documents changed. There were cases where such officials would be discovered and ousted from government service, only to find employment with some of the most prominent immigration attorneys in town.

Immigrants entering under false identities were often the able-bodied, male members of a family who were considered best suited to find employment in the United States. These male immigrants with false identity documents were commonly referred to as "paper sons." The Chinatowns of America have often been described as "Bachelor Societies," devoid of women and children. However, in reality, many Chinese men in America during the Exclusion era actually had wives and children residing in China.

Left behind in China, the wives of Chinese immigrants in the United States were referred to as "grass widows" or "living widows." Though they were married and assumed all the obligations of a wife, these women often led solitary lives separated from their husbands for years and even decades at a time. As a result, the normal formation of family life and community development both in the rural villages of China and the early Chinatowns of America suffered.

Legacy of Chinese Exclusion

The Chinese Exclusion Act was a pivotal point in U.S. immigration history. Its impact most definitely reverberated throughout the Asian Pacific region as the United States subsequently restricted and/or excluded immigrants of Japanese, Korean, Filipino, and Asian Indian descent. By executive agreement, statute, and eventually, by a key clause in the National Origins Act of 1924 (which barred all "aliens ineligible to citizenship"), America closed its doors to more and more immigrants for reasons of race, ethnicity, and country of origin.

It was not until 1943, when President Franklin D. Roosevelt was motivated by China's war efforts against Japan in World War II, that the Chinese Exclusion Act was finally repealed. In statements made at that time, the repeal was in recognition of those fighting valiantly in China, and clearly an attempt to diminish propaganda efforts on the part of Japan that painted America as racist.

However, as a result of strict quotas instituted under the National Origins Act of 1924, immigration was still severely restricted for the Chinese. Though primarily passed to limit immigration from eastern and southern Europe, and Russia, immigration quotas were now tied to a very small percentage based on U.S. Census figures of how many people from a certain country were living in the United States in 1890. This translated to only 105 Chinese a year being permitted to enter the United States. A later amendment to the law defined this restriction further by applying to those who were by blood 50% or more Chinese from anywhere in the world (versus just one country).

Later provisions permitted alien Chinese wives and minor children of domiciled alien merchants to enter outside of these harsh quotas. There was also the War Brides Act, which permitted Chinese (among others) serving in the U.S. armed forces to bring their wives. However, the real key to reversing immigration restrictions and allowing for meaningful family reunification did not occur until the Kennedy and Johnson administrations finally abolished ethnic quotas with the 1965 Immigration Act. A painful and epic period in U.S. history finally came to an end.

Viewpoint 8

"Massive immigration of a surplus and thus low-wage population vastly different culturally from Americans generated severe social conflicts across the entire range of society."

Immigration Laws That Discriminated Against Asians Were Appropriate

Otis L. Graham

Mining and railroad companies began importing thousands of Chinese laborers during the mid-1800s to perform backbreaking work for low wages. When the California gold rush ended and the transcontinental railroad was completed, the immigration of Chinese laborers was no longer necessary and the repressed hostility against Asians—Chinese and Japanese, who were also starting to immigrate to the United States in large numbers—came out into the open. Residents on the West Coast felt threatened by the Asians—by their large numbers, their willingness to work for low pay, and their racial and ethnic dif-

Otis L. Graham, "The Unfinished Reform: Regulating Immigration in the National Interest," *Debating American Immigration, 1882–Present*, edited by Roger Daniel and Otis L. Graham. Lanham, MD: Rowman & Littlefield, 2001. Copyright © 2001 by Rowman & Littlefield Publishers, Inc. Reproduced by permission.

ferences. Many Americans also believed that Chinese laborers' willingness to work for little pay was lowering wages for everybody. These complaints led to the first law restricting a class of people: the Chinese Exclusion Act of 1882.

In the following viewpoint, Otis L. Graham supports the restriction against Chinese immigration—despite some flaws in the act—as a necessary measure to protect the American labor market. In addition, Graham claims that the restriction allowed the tension and hostility between the Asians and white Americans to dissipate, thus avoiding the social conflict that was sure to erupt if Chinese immigration had not been restricted. Graham is professor emeritus at the University of California, Santa Barbara. Previously, he served as chairman of the board of the Center for Immigration Studies in Washington, D.C.

The long road to immigration reform began in an unlikely place—on the West Coast, with the question of the Chinese. Mine owners and railroad builders in the region, desperate for cheap and docile labor ready for backbreaking tasks, began importing Chinese coolie (the term was an English version of a Hindu phrase for unskilled laborers transported from the Orient) labor about 1850, along with a few females for prostitution. The reception of California citizens at first tended to be genial to the almost entirely male labor force, described by one citizen as "sober, industrious, and inoffensive." The reception turned hostile when at the end of the 1860s the gold rush boom had waned and the Union Pacific Railroad was completed (1869), but Asian immigration continued. Chinese numbers by the 1870s reached 10 percent of the state's population and one-quarter of its labor force, a low-wage labor pool beginning to compete with American labor. The specter of continuing and unlimited flows of Chinese peasant labor seemed to many to threaten more than a downward pressure on wages. "Transported and largely controlled by certain Chinese societies," John Higham writes, "they awakened fears of a new kind of slavery in a nation already convulsed by the struggle over African slavery."

Beyond posing a fundamental economic threat to American
workers, the Chinese were almost universally thought entirely
unassimilable for permanent settlement. They fled, or were sent
into virtual slavery, from a once-respected ancient civilization,
which by the mid–nineteenth century had fallen into the chaos of
civil war and banditry of the Taiping Rebellion (1851–64) with its
outward ripples of disorder. The American image of China, once
favorable, veered toward the view that this disintegrating empire,
and therefore its citizens, now had little to teach the civilized world
in the arts of government or civil society. In America the Chinese
kept strictly to themselves in their residential enclaves and to the
American eye retained peculiar customs and questionable health
standards, operating private courts of justice through their secret
societies or "tongs," which were also said to control gambling and
opium rings. The fact that Chinese migrating to Hawaii met with
far less cultural resistance and showed less ethnic isolation suggests that their "unassimilability" on the West Coast was at least
partially a result of their reception by white society. In any event,
resistance to their growing numbers mounted and occasionally
could become vicious. There were taxes on and boycotts of Chinese laundries and other businesses, community expulsions, and
even riots. Organized opposition to Chinese immigrants came
from a coalition of workers, small farmers and shop owners, en-
ergized by the harsh depression of the mid-1870s. Denis Kearney
of the California Workingmen's Party, composed substantially of
immigrants, mostly Irish, provided passionate, even angry lead-
ership behind the slogan "The Chinese must go!" Employers also
came in for harsh criticism for using the Chinese as pawns. Anti-
Chinese sentiment erupted also on the East Coast when significant numbers of Chinese laborers arrived, and some were used as
strikebreakers in Massachusetts and New Jersey.

In response to a remarkable intensity of complaint on the West
Coast that was increasingly shared nationwide (the platforms of
both political parties endorsed restriction of Chinese immigration
in 1876 and 1880), Congress moved rapidly toward an historic re-
versal of the tradition of laissez-faire in immigration matters. A
Chinese Exclusion Act in 1879 was vetoed because it violated the
Burlingame Treaty of 1868. The treaty was renegotiated, and Con-

gress by wide margins passed the Chinese Exclusion Act of 1882, suspending the admission of Chinese "laborers" for ten years. (Chinese "other than laborers" could legally come to the United States with Chinese government certificates, an odd form of control; in any event, Chinese were declared ineligible for citizenship.) It was the first sharp curtailment of immigration to America— colonial, state, and federal bars to the insane and "persons likely to become a public charge" kept out very few—and was extended with minor adjustments for sixty years, until 1943, when Chinese "exclusion" (which had never been total) was eased.

A New Era

A new tradition of restricting immigration through federal policy had begun. Unfortunately, it was a fumbling start on the road to national control over U.S. demographic destiny and the labor market. West Coast Americans' understandable concerns over an unlimited flow of cheap Asian labor had sometimes veered into panic or anger, leading on occasion to resorts to force against very peaceful invaders, with much racialist language harsh to the modern ear. In the public debate, the arguments for continuing the laissez-faire regime on national immigration were remarkably puny—a combination of sentimental invocations of the permanent and circumstances-ignoring claims of a heritage of "hospitality to all suppressed nationalities," along with the argument, candidly stated by the Reverend Henry Ward Beecher, that without the Chinese, we Americans would have "no race that will be willing to do what we call menial work." Against this, restrictionists built a compelling argument that swung huge majorities behind immigration reform. "We do not object to the Chinese because of their race or their language or their religion," editorialized a labor union journal, whose readers surely agreed only in part: "But we do object to an organized effort to introduce cheap laborers into the Republic."

Differences Lead to Friction

Even those who were initially hesitant to break with the nation's open door policy concluded that, in addition to the labor problem, Americans and Chinese were simply too different to permit large and sustained Oriental immigration with the resultant social conflict. "If they are brought rapidly, in large numbers, into any Western country, there will be unpleasant friction . . .", said University of Michigan President James Angell, who had led negotiations to rewrite the Burlingame Treaty. In the crisis, democratic government had a responsibility to respond to overwhelming majority opinion. "The public peace is disturbed," said respected Republican Senator George Edmunds of Vermont, "and if you can save it by giving time for reason to restore itself and passion to cool, is it not wise? . . . Then let us protect the Chinamen by having them hold up a little while. . . . While all mankind are of one kin . . . one destiny," the Chinese were very different in culture and religion, and "no republic can succeed that has not a homogenous population." Edmunds was one of many, observes historian Andrew Gyory, who "did not condemn the Chinese or call them inferior; he simply stressed their differentness."

Thus, a beginning had been made in the emotionally difficult transition from traditional laissez-faire toward immigration limits. In retrospect, and even to moderates at the time, some of the terms of the debate needlessly offended another nationality and stigmatized those of Chinese origins remaining in America. A drastic reduction in Chinese immigration could have been amply justified in terms of labor market impacts and problems of assimilation of Asian immigration on a vast scale, without slurs on foreigners, and without denying citizenship to those already here. The restrictionist impulse activated many who never learned this lesson.

Another lesson was not fully grasped. Massive immigration of a surplus and thus low-wage population vastly different culturally from Americans generated severe social conflicts across the entire range of society (with the exception of large employers, always eager for cheap labor without concern for social repercussions). Those conflicts arose from real as well as perceived economic, social, and cultural threats to standards achieved and cherished by the native population. People will react to these forces, as they should in a self-governing republic, and the formula for turning those responses hostile and lengthy is unresponsive government. The Chinese Exclusion Act, with its stupid title and other flaws apparent to people living a century later (and to some at the time), prevented what had been building as a massive and sustained immigration of Chinese laborers to Jin-shan—"the Golden Mountain"—with explosive potential. The U.S. government's first step toward controlling one of the uncontrolled forces tearing at the social fabric allowed the level of social conflict and accommodation between Caucasians and Chinese on the West Coast to slowly (too slowly for anyone's preference) drain away to be replaced by the Occidental-Oriental amity that generally prevailed on the West Coast in the latter half of the twentieth century.

The progressive reform impulse now moved on to a confrontation with the rest of the uncontrolled Great Wave, as reformers erratically searched for a national policy on immigration to replace the laissez-faire stance so inappropriate to the modern era. . . .

Looking Back

[An immigration restriction] policy that had such beneficial economic, social, and demographic impacts, especially upon the American working class, immigrants in America, and blacks, might expect favorable treatment in the history textbooks. This was so for a brief time, but modern histories are harsh. Why so? The restrictionist reform impulse was composed of two interwoven strands, a defensive sense of cultural-racial superiority, paired with a realistic calculation that the common good of the people already here required curbs on an unregulated mass flow. The second impulse was sound and produced beneficial policy reform. However, it has been entirely eclipsed in memory by a caustic denunciation of the first. Americans in the second half of the twentieth century have (laudably) repudiated the nation's historic operating racial assumptions, and now all we can or will hear in the earlier restrictionism are the discordant distinctions between preferred and, by implication or assertion, undesirable nationalities. The wiser of the immigration reformers anticipated this complaint and pleaded for a restrictionism justified only by the desire for like-mindedness, without invidious distinctions. They could not prevent some people from doing the right thing—curbing the numbers according to some rationale supported by public opinion—while expressing the wrong reasons.

There were blunders and misjudgments—as always—in the legislation. The 1908 Gentlemen's Agreement limiting Japanese immigration was unwisely repudiated and replaced by the explicit bar to "aliens in admissible to citizenship" in the law of 1924, despite abundant testimony before Congress that Japanese-Americans and Japan saw this as insulting on several levels. The words were code for "Japanese," because Chinese and Asian Indians had been excluded earlier. They implied that Japan was not carrying out her part of the earlier arrangement, and Congress must step in to exclude the Japanese also. Because Japanese immigration continued but at a low level under both the Gentleman's Agreement and the 1924 act, nothing was gained by the legislative rebuff. Indeed, a central flaw of Progressive Era thinking and policy on immigration, judging it not just from our own era but within their own context, was the refusal, despite strong counter-arguments, to expand citizenship to all those allowed to reside in the country, whatever their nationality. Limitation of foreign population flows was a proper goal. Barring from citizenship any group legally and permanently in residence, long after citizenship was extended to blacks by the Fourteenth Amendment (1867), was a sad error of most reformers (and the courts), headed otherwise in the right general direction.

Legislation, like sausage, has unsavory ingredients. Immigration restriction, with its flaws, was one of the many positive measures of the progressive reform era, which sought—with considerable success—to bring costly and disruptive social forces under democratic control.

CHAPTER 4

Looking Back at America's History of Immigration

✸ Chapter Preface

The founding fathers of the United States believed so strongly that all persons were created equal that they made this principle the basis of their complaint against King George III of England in the Declaration of Independence. While most Americans would like to think that they are fair and nonjudgmental toward those of other races, national origin, or religion, a review of American immigration policy shows that at times, Americans have been extremely xenophobic.

America's first immigrants were largely English, French, and Dutch, who came to the New World to settle colonies. Then, in the early nineteenth century, due to changing world circumstances, the composition of immigrants began to change. The number of Irish and German immigrants doubled, and then tripled. American residents were alarmed first of all by the magnitude of the number of new arrivals, as well the nationalities of the immigrants. Many Americans looked down on the Irish immigrants, considering them unclean. It was difficult to be hygienic, however, when living ten or twelve to a room without running water, heat, or cooking facilities. The Irish—who were usually poor and unskilled—had been forced to live in crowded, squalid conditions. The Irish were also accused of stealing American jobs because the immigrants would take whatever work they could find. For these reasons and others, Irish immigrants were denigrated and many employers refused to hire them, stating in their ads, "No Irish Need Apply."

A large number of German immigrants moved to rural areas so they could buy farms, but those who settled in cities lived, like other immigrants, in ethnic clusters, known as "Kleindeutschland" ("Little Germany"). But instead of working as unskilled laborers, the Germans often started their own businesses. Some common occupations were bakers, butchers, cigar makers, tailors, and cabinetmakers—occupations which were generally admired. However, Germans were also well known for brewing beer and owning saloons. The German attitude toward beer and alcohol in general was frowned upon by many of their more straitlaced neighbors and was perhaps responsible for provoking antagonistic feelings toward Germans by their neighbors. Religious differences also caused some Americans to distrust German immigrants. German Lutherans were more conservative than American Lutherans, and their disagreement over religious policies led to a permanent schism in the American Lutheran Church. In addition, German immigrants often insisted on teaching their children their lessons in German. It reached the point that the Nebraska legislature banned instruction in any language other than English in the state's schools. Despite these cultural differences of the Irish and Germans some rancorous feelings, the immigrants who came to the United States between the 1820s and 1860s did assimilate into American culture despite dour predictions that assimilation was impossible.

During the next great wave of immigration between the 1880s and 1920s, Americans became alarmed once again about the quality of immigrants coming to the United States. The Irish and Germans were now considered "old" immigrants, and former fears about them were being replaced by worries about the "new" immigrants from southern and eastern Europe. Many Americans were convinced that these Slavic and Latin immigrants were racially inferior to the northern and western Europeans (mainly British, German, Irish, and Scandinavian immigrants). The "swarthy" complexions of the southern and eastern Europeans led many to believe the Italians, Poles, Hungarians, Russians, and other Slavs, were not "white." It was widely believed that the white race was superior to all other races and that, therefore, the number of immigrants from the inferior, darker races should be sharply reduced. If the large numbers of inferior immigrants were allowed to continue entering the United States without restriction, the quality of future Americans was bound to suffer due to the miscegenation that was sure to occur.

Not all Americans were opposed to immigration, however. Many people believed that immigrants of all ethnicities—Irish, German, Italian, and Slavic, to name a few—provided immense benefits to the United States. They argued that the immigrants worked at jobs that few American laborers were willing to do. In

addition, the immigrants who came to the United States were usually the best and brightest their former country had to offer. Immigration was a difficult process that required stamina and
courage, desirable traits that could benefit the United States.
Those who supported immigration pointed out that the United
States had been receiving a diverse collection of immigrants for
hundreds of years; these immigrants had assimilated into American culture and made the United States the great country it is.

The arguments for and against immigration have changed little during the history of the United States. The authors in the following chapter discuss some of the historical aspects of immigration and whether the country was right to implement restrictions.

Viewpoint 1

"America's historic 'essential nature' . . . was highly specific—racially, religiously, culturally—right up until modern times."

The United States's Ethnic Foundation Was White, Anglo-Saxon, and Protestant

Peter Brimelow

Peter Brimelow is a British immigrant to the United States and a senior editor at *Forbes* and *National Review* magazines. The following viewpoint is an excerpt from his 1995 book *Alien Nation: Common Sense About America's Immigration Disaster.* Brimelow argues that, for centuries, the vast majority of immigrants to the United States were white Europeans. White, Anglo-Saxon, Protestant Europeans are the people that make up America's ethnic core, he asserts. When other groups of immigrants (such as Catholics, Slavs, or Asians) began to immigrate to the United States, nativists tried to protect America's historic ethnicity by passing restrictions to keep them out. It is entirely appropriate, Brimelow maintains, that Americans would want to ensure that their ethnic core remained white, Anglo-Saxon, and Protestant.

Peter Brimelow, *Alien Nation: Common Sense About America's Immigration Disaster.* New York: Random House, 1995. Copyright © 1995 by Peter Brimelow. Reproduced by permission.

Essay Question 2

Global interdependence will be the norm by the year 2000. In this country English will be just one of the many languages commonly spoken and more than half the population will be people of color. Comment on the environment in which you grew up; has it prepared you for these changes? What knowledge and skills do you need for the twenty-first century?

Admissions Essay, Tufts University, 1993

From time to time while struggling with this book, and earlier, while writing the humongous "Time to Rethink Immigration?" *National Review* cover story that preceded it, I've broken off to experience once again—it will be for such a short, short time—the inexpressible joy of changing my infant American son's dirty diaper.

Birthright Citizenship

Alexander James Frank Brimelow is an American although I was still a British subject, and his mother a Canadian, when he shot into the New York Hospital delivery room, yelling indignantly, one summer dawn in 1991. This is because of the Fourteenth Amendment to the U.S. Constitution. It states in part:

> All persons born or naturalized in the United States, and subject to the jurisdiction thereof, are citizens of the United States and of the State wherein they reside.

The Fourteenth Amendment was passed after the Civil War in an attempt to stop Southern states denying their newly freed slaves the full rights of citizens. But the wording is general. So it has been interpreted to mean that any child born in the United States is automatically a citizen. Even if its mother is a foreigner. Even if she's just passing through.

This "birthright citizenship" is by no means the rule among industrialized countries. Even if you are born in a manger, the Japanese, French and Germans say in effect, that still doesn't make you a bale of hay. The British used to have birthright citizenship, but in 1983 they restricted—requiring for example that one parent be a legal resident—because of problems caused by immigration.

I am delighted that Alexander is an American. However, I do feel slightly, well, guilty that his fellow Americans had so little choice in the matter.

But at least Maggy and I had applied for and been granted legal permission to live in the United States. There are currently an estimated 3.5 to 4 million foreigners who have just arrived and settled here in defiance of American law. When these illegal immigrants have children in the United States, why, those children are automatically American citizens too.

And right now, *two thirds* of the births in Los Angeles County hospitals are to illegal-immigrant mothers.

In fact, a whole minor industry seems to have been created by those twenty-eight words added to the U.S. Constitution. One survey of new Hispanic mothers in California border hospitals found that 15 percent had crossed the border specifically to give birth, of whom a quarter said that their motive was to ensure U.S. citizenship for their child. . . .

Contrary to the menacing assertion of the Tufts University admissions bureaucrats quoted at the head of this [selection], "people of color" will *not* be anything like half the American population in the year 2000. They will most likely be little more than a quarter. But the Tufts bureaucrats will get their wish, within the lifetime of my little son—*if, and only if,* current immigration policy continues.

Racists

Some of my American readers will be stirring uneasily at this point. They have been trained to recoil from any explicit discussion of race. *And anyone who says anything critical of immigration is going to be accused of racism.* This is simply a law of modern American political life.

When you write a major article in a national magazine, you in effect enter into a conversation with Americans. And part of the conversation I got into by writing my *National Review* cover story illustrated this law. It was a muttering match with Virginia Postrel, editor of the libertarian *Reason* magazine.

Virginia flipped out at the word *experiment,* and launched into a rendition of the pro-immigration moldy oldie "America Is an

Experiment That Works." (This often happens.) I pointed out gently that the experiment in question was *not* America—but instead the 1965 Immigration Act and its imminent, unprecedented, ethnic and racial transformation of America. She replied angrily in print:

> ... he [*me!*] thus defines authentic Americans not by their values or actions but by their blood. This is nonsense and, though I hate to use the term, profoundly un-American.

Thus Virginia, like many modern American intellectuals, is just unable to handle a plain historical fact: that the American nation has always had a specific ethnic core. And that core has been white.

A nation, of course, is an interlacing of ethnicity and culture. Individuals of any ethnicity or race might be able to acculturate to a national community. And the American national community has certainly been unusually assimilative. But nevertheless, the massive ethnic and racial transformation that public policy is now inflicting on America is totally new—and in terms of how Americans have traditionally viewed themselves, quite revolutionary. Pointing out this reality may be embarrassing to starry-eyed immigration enthusiasts who know no history. But it cannot reasonably be shouted down as "racist." Or "un-American.". . .

My son, Alexander, is a white male with blue eyes and blond hair. He has never discriminated against anyone in his little life (except possibly young women visitors whom he suspects of being baby-sitters). But public policy now discriminates against him. The sheer size of the so-called "protected classes" that are now politically favored, such as Hispanics, will be a matter of vital importance as long as he lives. And their size is basically determined by immigration.

Nativists

"Nativist!" This magic word is another exorcist's spell always cast against anyone who dares question current immigration policy. Clearly, in the minds of many immigration enthusiasts, nativists are no different than the Black Hundreds—the anti-Semitic gangs implicated in the pogroms that accelerated immigration from Czarist Russia at the turn of the [twentieth] century.

Well, to adapt the song "The Farmer and the Cowman" from the musical *Oklahoma!*:

I'd like to say a word for the nativists.

In very significant ways, this common view of them is a myth.

The nativists were genuine American originals: members of the Order of the Star-Spangled Banner, a secret patriotic society about which its members were instructed to deny knowledge—supposedly the origin of their famous nickname, the Know Nothings. Organizing themselves as the American party in the mid-1850s, they scored stunning but short-lived successes on the eve of the Civil War.

But the Know Nothings were far from an ignorant mob, as immigration enthusiasts, probably misunderstanding that nickname, tend to assume. Recent research has shown that they were a cross section of solid middle- and upper-middle-class citizens. And the Know Nothings *never actually proposed restricting immigration*— just that, in the words of the Know Nothing governor of Massachusetts, Henry J. Gardner, Americans should take care to "nationalize before we naturalize" any new immigrants. Nor were the Know Nothings anti-Semitic.

The Know Nothings were, however, deeply suspicious of Roman Catholicism—at a time when enormous Irish Catholic immigration had begun, after the potato famine of 1845.

Anti-Catholicism is not a sentiment you often find in America today (although you can get a whiff of it talking to abortion-rights and gay-rights activists). And it needs to be set in the context of the time. No doubt bigotry played a part. But so did a quite rational concern that Roman Catholicism with its hierarchical structure, unlike Judaism with its self-governing congregations, was not a "republican" religion—one that would be compatible with democracy, free institutions, law, liberty.

After all, Pope Pius IX was now fervently denouncing "liberalism," by which he meant all free thought and free institutions, and supporting the despotisms that had crushed liberal revolutions all across Europe in 1848. Indeed, in 1853, enraged native-born Americans and immigrant "Exiles of '48" united to riot against the visit of papal nuncio Gaetano Bedini, called "the Butcher of

Bologna" because of his role in suppressing the revolt against papal rule there.

Above all, *the Know Nothings were against slavery.* This stance was critical to their party's rise, when it provided a home for abolitionists disgusted with professional politicians' attempts to fudge the issue. And to its fall—forced to choose between abolition and nativism, the Know Nothings chose abolition. Most became Republicans. Several became famous in the Union army . . . notably its victorious general in chief, Ulysses S. Grant.

The nativists were not Nazis: they were nationalists—culturally and politically. They saw their American national identity as inextricably involved with what President John F. Kennedy, assimilated descendant of that Irish influx, would later call "the survival and success of liberty." Their concerns about immigration and slavery were different sides of the same coin. They may well have been overzealous. But their descendants need not feel ashamed of them.

And, incidentally, the Know Nothings left one enduring legacy: America's system of secular public schools. It was created largely in response to their concern about "nationalizing" immigrants. . . .

Myths About Immigration

With the opposition intimidated, immigration enthusiasts have been able to get away with treating American immigration history as a sort of Rorschach blot, into which they can read their personal preoccupations.

My current favorite is a [1994] cover story in *American Heritage* magazine (published by my own employer, *Forbes.* Harrumph!). After subtly linking me and my *National Review* article with French crypto-fascists and German neo-Nazis, the writer went on to proclaim:

> what is at stake here is nothing less than the essential nature of the United States of America . . . only the United States takes special pride in describing American nationality as, by definition, independent of race and blood—as something that is acquired by residence and allegiance regardless of birthplace or ancestry.

Of course this is absurd on its face: what about Australia and

Canada today? But . . . it is also ludicrously false as a description of America's historic "essential nature." This was highly specific—racially, religiously, culturally—right up until modern times, reinforced when necessary by legislation. For example, the first naturalization law, in 1790, stipulated that an applicant must be a "free white person." Blacks became full citizens only after the Civil War. Restrictions on Asians becoming citizens were finally dropped only after World War II. How much more specific can you get?

Maybe America should not have been like this. *But it was.*

Myth-manufacturing of this type amounts to an intellectual shell game—Americans (including, no doubt, many immigration enthusiasts themselves) are being tricked out of their own identity.

And it infests U.S. immigration history. Thus the lines now commemorated on a (surprisingly inconspicuous) plaque beneath the base of the Statue of Liberty

> . . . Give me your tired, your poor,
> your huddled masses yearning to breathe free,
> The wretched refuse of your teeming shore . . .

are not part of the Declaration of Independence or some other pronouncement of the Founding Fathers. Instead, they are the reaction of a young Zionist, Emma Lazarus, to the Russian pogroms following the assassination of Czar Alexander II in 1881. They were added years after the dedication of the statue, which was a gift from France to commemorate the U.S. centennial, predated the Ellis Island era of mass immigration, and was originally supposed to symbolize not "the Mother of Immigrants," in Lazarus's phrase, but *Liberty Enlightening the World*—"liberty *under law*," adds Federation for American Immigration Reform executive director Dan Stein, thinking grimly of recent amnesties for illegals.

And they aren't even true. American immigration has typically been quite selective, if only because the cost of passage was (until recently) an effective filter. Early English settlers included Royalist gentry who went to Virginia, like George Washington's ancestors, and Puritan gentry who went to New England, as Oliver Cromwell and his family once planned to do.

And, whatever the Know Nothings may have thought, the Irish immigrants swarming in after the 1845 potato famine were not the bottom of the barrel. Three quarters of them were literate; their fares were commonly paid by established extended families.

There are many other immigration myths. For example, immigration into the United States was never really completely free. There were always some restrictions. Immigration from Asia was cut off in the nineteenth century almost as soon as it began. And even European immigration was carefully monitored, for example to screen out potential paupers and threats to public health. Arguably, this scrutiny was actually stricter when immigration policy was the responsibility of the individual states, as it was until 1875.

And—this myth is really unkillable, no doubt because it so usefully frightens people from thinking about immigration policy— *the use of intelligence testing played no real role in the restrictive legislation passed in the 1920s.* Nor did intelligence testers ever allege that Jews and other immigrants of that period were disproportionately "feeble-minded." The claim that they did so is mainly based on what appears to be almost a wilful misreading of the work of the psychometric pioneer H.H. Goddard, which persists although it was exposed well [in the 1980s].

Common Sense About Immigration

The antidote to myth is common sense. This book [Brimelow's *Alien Nation: Common Sense About America's Immigration Disaster*] takes its subtitle from Thomas Paine's famous pamphlet *Common Sense*, the passionate argument for American independence from Britain that caused a sensation when it was published in early 1776.

There are some pleasing parallels here. Like me, Paine was an English immigrant—indeed, he had arrived in Philadelphia from England only just over a year before. But he still put on the American cause like a glove.

This is what it means to have a common political culture. In a real sense, the American Revolution was a civil war that split both peoples. Whole regiments of American Loyalists fought for the Crown; eight of the fifty-six signers of the Declaration of Independence were British-born. For Paine, the American Revolution was simply a transatlantic version of the radical cause in British politics.

Ironically in the context of my book, Paine himself is regularly cited by immigration enthusiasts because of his rhetorical conclusion that America should become "an asylum for mankind." Which just shows what happens when people don't read original sources. Earlier in *Common Sense*, Paine had made it clear that he was talking about asylum for *Europeans* ("we claim brotherhood with every European Christian"). And he explicitly grounded this claim on a common European culture distinct from that of the rest of the world. ("All Europeans meeting in America, or any other quarter of the globe, are *countrymen* . . ." [Paine's emphasis]).

Of course, I must modestly decline to make too much of the parallels between Paine and myself. Apart from anything else, he died a rather sad death, although not in poverty as is sometimes alleged, thanks to the generosity of the New York State government. (Another parallel I'm not holding my breath about.) And he was unmistakably a man of the Left, something I would hardly presume to claim.

As a radical, Paine had a political agenda—the break with Britain. And he read it into his account of the contemporary reality as gaily as any Tufts University Admissions bureaucrat. To minimize the link with Britain, he asserted that "Europe, and not England, is the parent country of America" and that "not one third of the inhabitants, even of this province, are of English descent."

In fact, although Pennsylvania was perhaps the least English of the Thirteen Colonies, in 1790 white Americans as a whole were 60 percent English, almost 80 percent British, 98 percent Protestant. (And, of course, some 20 percent of the population were voiceless black slaves.)

Paine's move is a common one in the immigration shell game. Thus an exhibit at the Ellis Island Museum of Immigration has a notice reading: "BY 1789, WHEN GEORGE WASHINGTON WAS IN-AUGURATED PRESIDENT, WE WERE ALREADY A MULTIETHNIC AND MULTI-RACIAL SOCIETY."

This assertion is a lie. It may be a "Noble Lie," the kind that the classical Greek philosopher Plato thought rulers should tell in order to keep their subjects happy. But it is still flagrantly false.

America at the time of the Revolution was biracial, not multi-racial, containing both whites and blacks. But the political nation—the collectivity that took political decisions—was wholly white. And that white nation was multiethnic only in the sense that a stew can be described as half-rabbit, half-horse if it contains one rabbit and one horse. There were a few unusual fragments in the American stew of 1790. But, for better or worse, it tasted distinctly British.

What About My Grandfather?

Many Americans have difficulty thinking about immigration restriction because of a lurking fear: *This would have kept my grandfather out. . . .*

But it must also be stressed: *that was then; this is now.* There are important differences between the last Great Wave of Immigration and today's.

> 1. Then, there was an "Open Door" (essentially—and with the major exception of the restriction on Asians). Now, the 1965 reform has reopened the border in a perversely unequal way. Essentially, it has allowed immigrants from some countries to crowd out immigrants from others.

The 1965 Immigration Act did not open the immigration floodgates: it opened the immigration scuttles—the influx is very substantial, but it spurts lopsidedly from a remarkably small number of countries, just as when some of the scuttles are opened in one side of a ship. Which is why the United States is now developing an ethnic list—and may eventually capsize. *Your grandfather probably couldn't get in now anyway.*

Viewpoint 2

"Only the United States takes special pride in describing American nationality as, by definition, independent of race and blood—as something that is acquired by residence and allegiance regardless of birthplace or ancestry."

The United States Does Not Have a National Ethnicity

Bernard A. Weisberger

Bernard A. Weisberger is a contributing editor to *American Heritage* magazine and the author of more than one dozen books about American history. In the following viewpoint, Weisberger asserts that the urge to restrict immigration to the United States is nothing new; it has been heard many times before in the country's history. He maintains that, although the original immigrants may have been primarily English, they have been supplemented with immigrants of all different ethnicities who have come to the United States and made their own contributions to their new country. The United States is unique among nations, Weisberger contends, in that American citizens are defined by their residence and loyalty to their country, not by their race or ethnicity.

Bernard A. Weisberger, "A Nation of Immigrants," *American Heritage*, vol. 45, February/March 1994. Copyright © 1994 by American Heritage, a division of Forbes, Inc. Reproduced by permission.

It's a politician's bromide—and it also happens to be a profound truth.

No war, no national crisis, has left a greater impress on the American psyche than the successive waves of new arrivals that quite literally built the country. Now that arguments against immigration are rising again, it is well to remember that every single one of them has been heard before. . . .

Restrictionism Is Back in Fashion

The question of what our policy toward the world's huddled masses should be is especially topical at this moment. The Statue of Liberty still lifts her lamp beside the golden door, but in a time of economic downturn, there is no longer an assured consensus that the door should be kept open very far. Restrictionism is back in fashion. For every journalistic article like that of *Business Week* in July 1992, which notes that "the U.S. is reaping a bonanza of highly educated foreigners" and that low-end immigrants "provide a hardworking labor force to fill the low-paid jobs that make a modern service economy run," there is another like Peter Brimelow's in the *National Review*. His title tells it all: "Time to Rethink Immigration?" The burden of his argument is that America has admitted too many immigrants of the wrong ethnic background (he himself is a new arrival from Britain), that neither our economy nor our culture can stand the strain, and that "it may be time to close the second period of American history [the first having been the era of the open frontier] with the announcement that the U.S. is no longer an 'immigrant country.'" In short, we're here; you foreigners stay home. Nor are journalists the only voices in the debate. In 1993, California's governor Pete Wilson got media attention with a proposal to amend the Constitution so as to deny citizenship to an entire class of people born in the United States, namely, those unlucky enough to be the children of illegal immigrants.

The United States Is Different

If, as I have, you have been "doing" immigration history for many years, you've heard the restrictionist arguments before and expect to hear them again. And you are under the obligation to answer back, because what is at stake in the argument is nothing less than the essential nature of the United States of America. We are different. We aren't the only country that receives immigration or that has to deal with resentment directed toward "aliens." The popularity in France of Jean-Marie Le Pen's National Front party and the surge of anti-foreign (and neo-Nazi) "Germany-for-Germans" violence in Germany are evidence of that. It's also true that in a world of swift intercontinental travel and instant global communication, immigration policy cannot really be made by separate governments as if they lived in a vacuum. Such problems as there are demand multinational solutions.

Nevertheless and notwithstanding, the United States of America is different. Immigration is flesh of our flesh, and we need to be reminded of that. Some sneer at the statement that we are a nation of immigrants as a cliché; all nations, they assert, are made up of mixtures of different peoples. So they are, as new tribes and races displaced old ones by conquest or by random immigration. But the United States was created by settlers who arrived from elsewhere, who deliberately and calculatedly invited and urged others to follow them, and who encouraged the process in ways that were unique. Of course, countries like Canada and Australia depended on immigration for survival and success, but only the United States made the acquisition of citizenship swift and simple; only the United States made it a matter of principle to equalize the conditions of new citizens and old; only the United States takes special pride in describing American nationality as, by definition, independent of race and blood—as something that is acquired by residence and allegiance regardless of birthplace or ancestry.

Confirmation of that statement is in the record, and the record needs to be reviewed. It is not a flawless one. Of course the people of the United States have not always extended an equal welcome to all races; of course there have been spasms of hostility like the current wave—in the 1790s, in the 1850s, in the 1920s. They are also part of the record, but on the whole the record is exceptional and ought to be known and understood before any new major changes in policy are made. . . .

Now is the proper occasion for retelling the immigration story.

So let us begin at the beginning, with the statement that offends the new exclusionist.

In the Beginning: 1607–1798

"We are a nation of immigrants." It's a politician's generality at an ethnic picnic, a textbook bromide swallowed and soon forgotten. It is also, as it happens, a profound truth, defining us and explaining a good part of what is extraordinary in the short history of the United States of America. There is no American ancient soil, no founding race, but there is a common ancestral experience of moving from "there" to "here." Among the founders of this nation who believed that they were agents of destiny was an English preacher who said in 1669, "God hath sifted a nation that he might send choice grain into this wilderness." The grain has arrived steadily and from many nations. "Americans are not a narrow tribe," wrote Herman Melville; "our blood is as the flood of the Amazon, made up of a thousand noble currents all pouring into one."

We begin arbitrarily with a seventeenth-century English migration that produced the First Families of Virginia (founded in 1607) and Massachusetts's Pilgrim Fathers (1620). Arbitrarily because already in 1643 Isaac Jogues, a French Jesuit missionary visiting New Amsterdam, said he heard eighteen languages spoken in that seaport town, which probably included Mediterranean and North African dialects and the Hebrew of a small settlement of Sephardic Jews.

But the stock planted in the 1600s was basically English. In the eighteenth century it turned "British" as Scots and Irish arrived in significant numbers, then partly European through an influx of Germans, and African, too, through the thousands of involuntary black immigrants brought in on the hell ships of the slave trade.

Those initial colonial migrations to "British North America" illustrate forces that are still at work in 1993. The names, faces, and languages change, but the basics remain. Immigrants are pushed out of their original homes by war, upheaval, misery, and oppression. They are pulled toward America by the promise of economic betterment and a chance to breathe free. Sometimes they are lured by promoters who want their passage money or their labor and skills. Sometimes they have come in legal or actual bondage.

But whenever and wherever they have come, they have changed what they found. . . .

Young Republic, 1815–1860

[Thomas] Jefferson's optimistic vision of an always enlightened and open-minded America has survived as a hotly contested influence on the land. But his expectation that the nation would remain permanently agrarian was totally wrong. Half a century after he left the White House, steam power had transformed the country. Inventors and investors proved the truest American radicals. Steamboats and rail lines crisscrossed a Union that spread to the Pacific and boasted more than thirty states. Mills, mines, factories, distilleries, packinghouses, and shipyards yearly churned out millions of dollars' worth of manufactured goods.

And it was linked to mass immigration. Immigrants furnished much of the labor that made the productive explosion possible and many of the consumers who made it profitable. The same industrializing processes that were at work and opened jobs here uprooted millions in Europe whose handicrafts became obsolete or whose land fell into the hands of those who could farm more "efficiently." Two decades of Napoleonic warfare, followed by three more of suppressed democratic and nationalist revolution, created a new reservoir of suffering from which emigration offered an escape.

America was a major beneficiary. Europe's growing cities and new overseas dominions beckoned, but the United States was the special promised land as the nineteenth century took its dynamic course.

The Irish Migration

Fewer than 8,000 immigrants per year landed on American shores between 1783 and 1815, but 2,598,000 came in the next forty-five years: 1,500,000 in the 1840s and 3,000,000 in the 1850s. The pre–Civil War period of immigration belonged predominantly to 1,500,000 Germans and 2,000,000 Irish. It was the Irish whose transplantation was most shadowed in tragedy. Unbelievably, Ireland—only a few hours by water from the very center of the modern world in England—was stricken by the oldest of Biblical scourges, famine.

Irish migration had begun early. The rich English absentee land-lords who ruled the country left their peasant tenants to feed themselves on the potatoes grown on tiny plots. A visitor declared that "the most miserable of English paupers" was better off. Irish Catholics and Irish nationalists were equally despised and frustrated. There was little future, and thousands, early in the century, migrated to the United States to find pick-and-shovel jobs on the growing network of turnpikes, canals, and railroads. But in 1845 the stream of opportunity seekers was turned into a flood of refugees. The potato crop, smitten by a fungus, failed in three successive years. Mass starvation was the result. In the hovels inhabited by the "Paddies," rats gnawed on unburied bodies while others in their death throes looked on, too weak to move. "All with means are emigrating," wrote one official; "only the utterly destitute are left behind."

Victims of the "Great Hunger" were not through with their torments when they boarded filthy, overcrowded, and underprovisioned ships, where, said one witness, it was "a daily occurrence to see starving women and children fight for the food which was brought to the dogs and pigs that were kept on deck." En route 10 to 20 percent of them died of disease. In the United States, lacking capital and prepared only for low-level employment, they were crammed into the new urban slums. Some were housed, according to an investigation committee, nine in a room in windowless and waterless cellars, "huddled together like brutes without regard to age or sex or sense of decency."

The Germans

It was a little better for the Germans. Many were professionals and scholars with some capital, political refugees rather than disaster victims. Some came in groups that pooled their money to buy cheap Western lands, and these founded towns like New Ulm in Minnesota or New Braunfels in Texas. So many of them became Texans, in fact, that in 1843 the state published a German edition of its laws. An American reporter visited a German farm in Texas in 1857. "You are welcomed," he told readers, "by a figure in a blue flannel shirt and pendant beard, quoting Tacitus, having in one hand a long pipe, in the other a butcher's knife; Madonnas upon log-walls; coffee in tin cups upon Dresden saucers; barrels for seats to hear a Beethoven's symphony on the grand piano."

German farmers spread through Illinois, Michigan, Missouri, Iowa, and Wisconsin. German brewers, bookbinders, butchers, musicians, and other craftspeople settled cohesively and proudly in cities from New York to New Orleans, St. Louis to Cincinnati. In 1860, 100,000 New York Germans supported twenty churches, fifty German-language schools, ten bookstores, five printing establishments, and a theater, in neighborhoods known collectively as Kleindeutschland (little Germany). To contemporaries the Germans seemed a model minority, the Irish a problem minority—a kind of generalizing that would, in time, be transferred to other peoples.

Besides these two major groups, there were Danes, Norwegians, and Swedes arriving in increasing numbers from the 1850s onward; French-Canadians moving into New England textile factories to replace Yankee workers of both sexes; Dutch farmers drifting to western Michigan; and in 1849 Chinese who had heard of the California gold strikes and came for their share of the "Golden Mountain," as they called America—only to be crowded out of the mining camps by mobs and restrictive laws and diverted into railway labor gangs, domestic service, restaurants, and laundries.

The immigrants helped push the United States population from 4,000,000 in 1790 to 32,000,000 in 1860. They built America by hand, for wages that were pittances by modern standards—$40 a month in Pennsylvania coal mines, $1.25 to $2 a day on the railroads—but tempting nonetheless. (In Sweden farmhands earned $33.50 per year.) They dug themselves into the economy and into the nation's not-always-kindly ethnic folklore. New England textile towns like Woonsocket and Burlington got to know the accent of French-Canadian "Canucks." So many Swedes became Western lumbermen that a double-saw was called a "Swedish fiddle." Welsh and Cornish copper miners in Michigan's Upper Peninsula were known as Cousin Jacks.

There were exceptions to the geographical stereotypes—Dutch settlements in Arizona, a Swedish nucleus in Arkansas, a Chinese community in Mississippi—and Irishmen in Southern cities like Mobile and New Orleans, where they were employed on dangerous jobs like levee repair because they were more expendable than fifteen-hundred-dollar slaves.

American culture shaped itself around their presence. Religion was a conspicuous example. The Church of Rome in America was turned inside out by the Irish, whose sheer numbers overwhelmed the small groups of old-stock English and French Catholics from Maryland and Louisiana. The first American cardinal, John Mc-Closkey, was the son of a Brooklyn Irishman. The second, James Gibbons, an Irish boy from Baltimore. German and Swiss Catholic immigrants added to the melting-pot nature of their church in the United States before the Civil War—and the Poles and Italians were yet to come. . . .

The Rise of Nativism

But the lower-class Irish in particular stung an American elite long steeped in anti-popery. Anti-immigrant feelings began to rise in the 1840s and focused especially on the Irish, who, like poor people before and after them, were denounced for not living better than they could afford. "Our Celtic fellow citizens," wrote a New York businessman, "are almost as remote from us in temperament and constitution as the Chinese." Bigotry can always find excuses and weapons. The handiest one in the 1840s was anti-Catholicism.

In 1834 a Boston mob burned a convent. Ten years later there were riots in Philadelphia after a school board ruled that Catholic children might use the Douay version of the Bible in school. "The bloody hand of the Pope," howled one newspaper, "has stretched itself forth to our destruction." A few years after that, anti-Catholic and anti-foreign feelings merged in a nativist crusade called the Know-Nothing movement. Its goal was to restrict admission and naturalization of foreigners, and among its adherents was Samuel F.B. Morse, the father of telegraphy, who cried aloud: "To your posts! . . . Fly to protect the vulnerable places of your Constitution and Laws. Place your guards. . . . And first, shut your gates."

Know-Nothings had some brief success but little enduring impact. Their drive got strength from a generalized anxiety about the future of the country on the eve of the Civil War. But Know-Nothingism cut across the grain of a venerable commitment to equal rights, and no one put his finger on the issue more squarely than Abraham Lincoln when asked in 1855 whether he was in favor of the Know-Nothing movement: "How could I be? How can any one who abhors the oppression of negroes, be in favor of degrading classes of white people? Our progress in degeneracy appears to me to be pretty rapid. As a nation, we began by declaring that 'all men are created equal.' We now practically read it, 'all men are created equal, except negroes.' When the Know-Nothings get control, it will read, 'all men are created equal, except negroes, and foreigners and catholics.' When it comes to this I should prefer emigrating to some country where they make no pretence of loving liberty—to Russia, for instance, where despotism can be taken pure, and without the base alloy of hypocrisy."

Three years later, on the Fourth of July, 1858, in debating with Stephen A. Douglas, Lincoln returned to the theme. What could the Fourth mean, he asked, to those who were not blood descendants of those who had fought in the Revolution? His answer was that in turning back to the Declaration of Independence, they found the sentiment "We hold these truths to be self-evident, that all men are created equal," that they "feel . . . and that they have a right to claim it as though they were blood of the blood, and flesh of the flesh of the men who wrote that Declaration and so they are. That is the electric cord . . . that links the hearts of patriotic and liberty-loving men together."

Lincoln was unambiguous. There was no exclusively American race entitled to claim liberty by heredity. What held the nation together was an idea of equality that every newcomer could claim and defend by free choice.

That concept was soon tested to the limit with Lincoln himself presiding over the fiery trial. Foreign-born soldiers and officers served the Union in such numbers and with such distinction that the war itself should have laid to rest finally the question of whether "non-natives" could be loyal. It didn't do that. But it paved the way for another wave of economic growth and a new period of ingathering greater than any that had gone before.

Viewpoint 3

"Immigrants did not dissolve culturally on contact with America, and they did not cease entirely to be Italians or Croatians or Russian Jews."

Immigrants Did Not Assimilate Well

L. Edward Purcell

Immigrants share similar experiences despite the fact that they arrived in the United States during different eras, asserts L. Edward Purcell in the following viewpoint. Although many like to argue that America is a "melting pot" in which immigrants immerse themselves and emerge as Americans without recognizable signs of their ethnic heritage, Purcell contends that this is a false belief. Immigrants tended to settle together in ethnic or national enclaves. This allowed them to retain at least some aspects of their ethnic identity—language, culture, or customs—for at least two generations and sometimes into the third or fourth generation. Purcell is an independent historian, editor, and journalist who has written more than a dozen books and numerous articles, many of them on historical topics.

The social process of immigration involves how immigrants assimilate, how they maintain their ethnic identities, how their religion changes, and how they behave politically. Historians and

L. Edward Purcell, *Immigration*. Phoenix, AZ: Oryx, 1995. Copyright © 1995 by L. Edward Purcell. Reproduced by permission of Greenwood Publishing Group, Inc., Westport, CT.

social scientists now believe that the social process immigrants experienced after arriving in America was remarkably similar from place to place and from decade to decade. Even immigrant experiences that seem widely different on the surface share certain basic characteristics according to this viewpoint. In short, all immigrants bring with them cultural and social patterns from their previous homes, and within a brief span these patterns are altered by exposure to the new environment of America. At the same time, these cultural and social patterns have an impact on America. This two-way effect was as true for an indentured servant in 17th-century Virginia as for a Norwegian farmer in late 19th-century Minnesota. It was also certainly true of the great masses of immigrants who arrived in America between 1880 and 1920.

Furthermore, it is very important—as observers have recently pointed out—to understand that immigrants from the turn of the [twentieth] century were not passive victims who were torn from former lives and thrust into a bewildering new world. On the contrary, all immigrants (save, perhaps, political refugees) were people who had taken active control of their lives.

In short, they chose to emigrate, to leave the old behind and embrace the new. Far from being victims, immigrants at the turn of the century were examples of courage and determination. They not only sought change, but dealt with it well once in their new homes.

At the height of the flood tide of immigration, the English-Jewish playwright Israel Zangwill's 1908 play "The Melting Pot" first popularized the idea that the new immigrants would find themselves in a process by which all alien people would be recast by contact with America and older American groups so that an entirely new kind of person would emerge.

This idea spread quickly as an interpretation of immigration and had considerable charm for older Americans, most of whom wanted the newcomers to change as quickly as possible into something more recognizable than transplanted eastern or southern European peasants or *shtetl* dwellers. It also had some attraction for many immigrants, those who rapidly tired of being on the bottom of the economic ladder and outside the system of social acceptance in America.

The melting pot idea, of course, supposed that immigrants would be transformed into "good" Americans but America would only be affected to a small degree by the culture of the immigrants.

In retrospect, it is clear that the entire concept of a melting pot was erroneous. Immigrants did not dissolve culturally on contact with America, and they did not cease entirely to be Italians or Croatians or Russian Jews, at least in the sense of how they understood the world and how they wanted the world to accept them. Moreover, America was certainly not immune to changes caused by the presence of millions of new people. Even kinsmen and fellow countrymen who had come earlier were unable to resist the changes brought by the new immigrants: German and Sephardic Jews, for example, found the Russian Jews perturbed and unsettled their lives.

A Clash Between Old and New

That a clash would take place between old and new was, perhaps, inevitable. Older Americans, including many who were themselves relatively recent immigrants or the children or grandchildren of recent immigrants, organized social movements to alleviate some of the economic hardships of the new immigrants and to begin the process of "Americanization," attempting to strip away the alien culture and assimilate the newcomers into the mainstream of traditional American society. Just after the turn of the century, the Americanization movement was spearheaded by urban social workers who saw at close range the effects of immigrant poverty and poor living conditions. The movement soon took on a note of urgency that came from supporters who wanted to enforce social unity on a nation they saw in danger of falling into a chaotic diversity. State agencies as well as volunteer organizations were pressed into this effort, and they attempted to educate the immigrants to the basics of the "American way" from hygiene . . . to ideology. When America entered World War I, the Americanization effort took on even more importance and became a bulwark of what was all too often overzealous patriotism.

Interestingly, the Americanizers' dreams of assimilation were seldom realized, at least not among the first generation of immigrants. The old ways persisted and could not be suppressed by persuasion and propaganda. People could not and did not give up their identities just because they had decided to move to America. Almost all the immigrant groups at the turn of the century persisted in using their native languages, for example (as had previous non-English speaking immigrants from the 17th century on), and they found numerous ways of recreating or sustaining their social customs. Folkways that had been transparently adapted from native lands found places in the immigrant communities of America, and many have been sustained for a century or more as a way to remind immigrants of their original identity.

During the early years, however, the immigrant's ethnic or national identity was reinforced daily by the settlement patterns of most immigrants. The great majority of the immigrants who arrived between 1880 and 1920 lived together in ethnic and national enclaves. Whether in New York's crowded Lower East Side, less intense neighborhoods in other cities across the land, or rural midwestern Scandinavian "ghettos," the new immigrants formed identifiable clusters. They lived in boarding houses with their fellow countrymen, and they socialized in taverns or coffee houses where their own languages were spoken and their customs catered to.

The impact of the immigrants was certainly greatest in the cities, however, and the influx of so many millions in such a short time altered the urban landscape of America. Many cities—Chicago and New York are only the most prominent examples—achieved an astonishing mixture of peoples almost overnight. Moving through the dense immigrant sections of a city presented a kaleidoscope of language, dress, and customs.

Although later research has shown that few ethnic immigrant enclaves achieved anything close to a 100 percent solidarity, the effect of urban living patterns at the time was spectacular. Neighborhoods appeared to be completely Jewish or Italian or Greek or Polish and were disorienting for the visitor. An often-cited example of the confusing mixture is the industrial town of Lawrence, Massachusetts, where it was said that around 1912 there were 25 nationalities and 45 languages or dialects.

Moreover, far too many of the immigrant districts were slums of the most vicious kind, a relatively new phenomenon in American urban life, at least on the scale achieved in the decades of highest immigration. The newcomers had slim resources and had to live wherever they could afford, and there were always landlords willing to create the most profitable rental housing, without regard for squalor or concern for the occupants. Many older Americans were shocked by the revelations of books like Danish immigrant Jacob Riis's *How the Other Half Lives* in 1890 and the report of the Dillingham Commission that conditions had only gotten worse 20 years later. Slums were apparently a consistent part of the lives of recent immigrants, whether in New York, the industrial cities of the Midwest, or the mining camps of more isolated regions.

In the cities, ethnic neighborhoods often presented a sort of running anthropological graph of change over time: because housing was cheapest in such neighborhoods, they attracted the newest arrivals, who in turn pushed out those who had come before. For example, Irish neighborhoods established 40 or 50 years earlier as the home of the working Irish immigrant poor became centers of Italian or Jewish life by the turn of the century—the Irish having reached a relative prosperity were ready and able to move to more expensive and diffused places.

Typically, however, changes showed up in the children of the immigrants. The second generation of almost all the major immigrant groups at the turn of the century reacted to the effects of their double environment—heavily ethnic at home but multicultural outside—and were transformed into "hyphenates"—Italian-Americans, Slovene-Americans, Greek-Americans, etc. The second generation usually failed to learn or at least to use the mother tongue of their parents, and exposure to the "outside" world in the public schools often produced a skepticism about the absolute value of their immigrant heritage. While the second generation fought to free itself from the confines of an exclusive immigrant heritage, it nonetheless maintained an inescapable connection. Even into the third and fourth generations, the offspring of immigrants demonstrate at least some form of direct connection, even if it be only an occasional community ritual or family observance, and among several ethnic groups the third or fourth generations have sponsored cultural revivals, including renewed interest in study of original languages.

Viewpoint 4

"The United States . . . has forged a culturally unified nation, hundreds of millions strong, spanning a continent, at peace with itself, out of people drawn, literally, from every corner of the earth."

Immigrants Assimilated Well

Peter D. Salins

Peter D. Salins argues in the following viewpoint that immigrants to the United States may have spoken a language other than English at home, ate ethnic foods, and celebrated their ethnic heritage, but they proudly considered themselves and their children to be Americans. Americans welcomed immigrants if they spoke English, took pride in their American identity and American ideals, and worked hard, he asserts. Furthermore, Salins maintains, the United States helped immigrants assimilate by offering them full citizenship, which gave them all the rights and privileges of being an American, and by educating their children in free public schools. Salins is a professor of urban affairs and planning at Hunter College of the City University of New York and is a senior fellow of the Manhattan Institute. He is also the author of *Assimilation, American Style*, from which the following viewpoint is excerpted.

Peter D. Salins, *Assimilation, American Style*. New York: BasicBooks, 1997. Copyright © 1997 by BasicBooks, a division of HarperCollins, Inc. Reproduced by permission.

My parents immigrated to the United States from Germany as young adults in 1938. We spoke German at home and ate German foods. My parents socialized with other German immigrants and joined German organizations. But not for one second during my German-speaking childhood did any of us—my parents, my sister, or I—doubt our Americanness. We took our Americanness for granted and were proud to be Americans. My national ancestors were not Otto von Bismarck or Frederick the Great, but George Washington and Thomas Jefferson. I thought *Father Knows Best* was about my family.

Ethnic, but Still American

The town in central New Jersey where I grew up could have served as the model for a series of Norman Rockwell paintings. But actually, most of my classmates' parents were foreign born, having come mainly from Italy and Poland. Did any of the kids I went to school with feel any the less American? Did they have conflicted ethnic loyalties? Absolutely not.

I also have friends who grew up in much more intensively ethnic enclaves—Italian, Russian, Middle Eastern, Cuban, and Chinese—in New York and other large cities. Their neighborhoods were replete with ethnic stores, restaurants, and social clubs, and few adults spoke English. They were invariably called "little" this or "little" that—fill in the ethnic blank. Like me, my friends spoke a foreign language at home, for their parents clung to most of their original folkways, and, culturally, lived in a world suspended somewhere between their birthplaces and the United States. But these young people grew up feeling every bit as American as I did. They accepted, perhaps even cherished, their Italian, Jewish, or other ethnic heritage, but they were proud to be Americans.

The story of my childhood may well strike the average reader as banal because we Americans take for granted that the immigrants of yesterday produced the Americans of today. And yet, assimilation, American style is more than just a historical artifact; it is nothing less than a miracle. For over two hundred years the United States has managed to pull off an almost impossible feat: It has forged a culturally unified nation, hundreds of millions strong, spanning a continent, at peace with itself, out of people drawn, literally, from every corner of the earth.

Ethnic Harmony Is Not Easy

To maintain and deepen a sense of national cultural unity amid ethnic diversity has not been a simple task or one that other nations have easily accomplished. Canada, for example, has never been able to resolve the terms of coexistence between its two principal ethnic groups, both of which are northern European. One hundred and thirty years after its independence, Canada is, in most respects, an agreeable, prosperous, freedom-loving country, but it teeters on the edge of dissolution.

In the Eastern Hemisphere things are much worse. Eastern Europe is a cauldron of ethnic hatreds from the Adriatic to the Urals. Long-united and almost ethnically indistinguishable Czechs and Slovaks recently split apart peacefully, but long-united and almost ethnically indistinguishable Yugoslavs are still splitting not so peacefully. Russians have been engaged in a devastating war with secessionist Chechens. Elsewhere in the former Soviet Union, one finds ethnic blood feuds among Georgians, permanent warfare between Armenians and Azerbaijanis, and long-resident Russians expelled from the Baltic states.

Even Western Europe harbors festering ethnic discord—in some cases among ancient ethnic antagonists, but in others, between natives and immigrants. The bitter conflict between Protestants and Catholics in Northern Ireland may be the most bloody, but there are countless examples of ongoing low-level ethnic discord. Greeks and Turks in Cyprus will never be reconciled. Flemish- and French-speaking Belgians maintain an uneasy ethnic truce that is dependent on formulas of power sharing and zones of influence. Italy is burdened with a north-south split that is at bottom ethnic, unhappy German-speaking South Tyrolians in Alto Adige, and discontented Slovenians and Croats in recently annexed Trieste. In Germany, working-class youths torch the homes of eastern European immigrants, and the country's naturalization policy denies citizenship to German-born descendants of Turkish guest workers who settled there more than thirty years ago. In France, the presence of large colonies of Islamic North

Africans periodically triggers social unrest and prompts xeno-phobic political campaigns. Nor should one forget that only fifty years ago, a European power went on a genocidal ethnic rampage in which millions lost their lives. And this is the "good news" part of the world. In India, Sri Lanka, and many nations of Africa, eth-nic conflict gives rise to unspeakable atrocities, unimaginable hu-man suffering, year after year. The brutal images of Rwanda and Somalia are more often the rule than the exception.

Americanization

Ethnic harmony is a fragile thing, and nations must work hard to maintain it. Thus, America's success as a multiethnic society is not simply a happy accident. As a country built on perpetual immi-gration, the United States has been struggling with the mission of maintaining national cultural and civic unity alongside ethnic di-versity since colonial times. Throughout the nineteenth and early twentieth centuries, both the elites and the rank and file of "na-tive" Americans aggressively and self-consciously promoted the idea of *assimilation*, or as they called it in the early years of [the twentieth] century, "Americanization." Just as the Constitution of the United States was designed to create a unified, functional na-tional society while preserving a maximum degree of individual liberty, so did its paradigm of assimilation aspire to the idea of *E Pluribus Unum*. (This Latin motto, "from many, one" is as old as the nation; it was chosen by a committee of the Continental Con-gress for the Great Seal of the United States and was adopted on June 20, 1782.)

Assimilation, American style set out a simple contract between the existing settlers and all newcomers. Immigrants would be wel-come as full members of the American family if they agreed to abide by three simple precepts: First, they had to accept English as the national language. Second, they were expected to take pride in their American identity and believe in America's liberal dem-ocratic and egalitarian principles. Third, they were expected to live by what is commonly referred to as the Protestant ethic (to be self-reliant, hardworking, and morally upright). This basic framework, though minimal, proved highly effective. Since culture is trans-mitted by language, a single common language worked as a powerful force for cultural unity. Faith in the American Idea, a unique, idealistic, and politically advanced set of liberal principles and institutions, promoted civic unity and national pride. The Protestant ethic, a belief system that judges individuals by their achievements, rather than by the circumstances of their birth, made ethnicity less relevant and united all Americans in a framework of shared values.

Citizenship

To seal the assimilation contract, immigrants were not only permitted, but encouraged to become citizens. The offer of citizenship was an advanced and radical idea in the eighteenth century, and even today most countries, if they accept immigrants at all, merely allow them to be residents, or second-class citizens at best. According to Craig Whitney of the *New York Times:* "In Germany, it can be easier for a child whose family lived in Russia for 200 years to become a German citizen than it is for . . . the German-born child of a Turkish 'guest worker' [because] Germany defines citizenship by bloodline." The United States, in contrast, always made immigrants eligible for a citizenship that conferred on them full membership in the American state and society, with all attendant rights and privileges (save one—the right to run for and be elected president).

To help implement the assimilation contract, most immigrant children were enrolled in free state-supported systems of public schools. The United States was one of the first nations to provide universal, compulsory, and free public education. As early as 1785, the federal government gave states land for public schools, and Massachusetts established the first free statewide public school system in the 1850s. The public school movement was driven by the egalitarian desire to instill knowledge and civic virtue in all Americans, regardless of wealth or class. But, as the educational reformer Horace Mann persuasively argued, public schools were necessary, above all, to ensure the assimilation of immigrants. Public school curricula were designed as much to acculturate immigrants and rural natives to the common values and demands of American society as they were to impart traditional learning. Schools fostered universal literacy and fluency in the English language. They explained and extolled the American Idea. They established norms of conduct, expectations, and attitudes. They fostered interethnic, interclass, and immigrant-native socialization.

It Worked

And it worked. This pervasive paradigm of assimilation served to unify the expanding population of the United States. Notwithstanding periodic bursts of nativism, faith in the paradigm made ordinary Americans willing to tolerate large-scale immigration. And as immigrants abided by the rules, Americans' faith in the paradigm was vindicated. At the same time, there was nothing especially coercive about the assimilation contract. All immigrants were free to be as ethnic as they pleased, especially at home or in their local communities. As the sociologist Richard Alba observed, "Assimilation need not imply the obliteration of all traces of ethnic origins, nor require that every member of a group be assimilated to the same degree." From colonial times to the present, millions of these assimilated Americans from other lands have lived in their own ethnic enclaves, eaten ethnic foods, and even spoken their original languages. There is really no inconsistency between America's aggressive promotion of assimilation and its tolerance of ever-changing ethnic diversity. The assimilation contract, with its three ground rules, was the unofficial law of the land well into the 1950s, and it was clearly in play during my formative years.

For Further Discussion

Chapter 1

1. After reading the viewpoints by the Native American Party and the *New York Mirror*, list what you think were Americans' primary concerns about immigrants of the early and mid-nineteenth century. List some of the facts these authors used to validate their concerns.

2. What are the main facts presented by Thomas L. Nichols and *Putnam's Monthly* to refute the idea that immigrants endanger American society?

3. John F. Kennedy writes, "Every American who ever lived, with the exception of one group, was either an immigrant himself or a descendant of immigrants." Other authors argue that the United States is not a nation of immigrants because only a small percentage of Americans are actually immigrants; the rest are their descendants. In your opinion, is the United States a nation of immigrants? Support your answer using examples from the viewpoints.

Chapter 2

1. One continuing fear of people already established in the United States was that the continual influx of immigrants would lower wages. Which author in this chapter do you think addresses this issue more convincingly? Why? Do you think the authors' backgrounds had any influence on their viewpoints? Explain your answer.

2. Advocates for restrictions on immigration used the same argument for every wave of immigrants: The immigrants were unskilled, illiterate, and incapable of assimilating into American culture. How do opponents of restrictions on immigration counter these arguments?

Chapter 3

1. E.W. Gilliam and George F. Seward disagree about whether the Chinese should be permitted to immigrate to the United

States. In their arguments, however, they use some of the same points to support opposite conclusions. On what points do they agree? How does Gilliam attempt to sway his readers to his point of view? Whose argument is more persuasive? Explain your answer.

2. Otis L. Graham admits that the restrictions against the Chinese were discriminatory and regrets their racist language, but he argues that the restrictions were necessary to prevent Asian immigrants from overwhelming the United States. Based on your reading of the viewpoints in this book, do you think his argument is valid? Why or why not?

Chapter 4

1. From your reading of this chapter, what seem to be the main reasons some Americans wanted to place restrictions on immigration? In your opinion, were these reasons altruistic or self-serving? Explain.

2. Several different kinds of restrictive legislation are discussed in this book. Based on your readings, are the restrictions based mainly on racist attitudes, limitations of the country's resources, or other ideas? Explain your answer.

3. Peter D. Salins and L. Edward Purcell use the same examples of immigrants living in the United States to come to opposite conclusions about whether immigrants are able to assimilate into American society. Which author do you think makes the strongest case? Why?

✳ Chronology

1600s

The English settle the eastern seaboard from Maine to Georgia; they are joined by smaller communities of Scots, French, Dutch, Spanish, Germans, and Swedes.

1607

England establishes the first permanent European settlement in the future United States at Jamestown, Virginia.

1700s

Large numbers of English, Scots, and Scotch Irish immigrants settle in America; fewer immigrants come from other European countries.

1776

The United States declares its independence from Great Britain.

1795

Congress passes the Naturalization Act, which requires a five-year residence in the United States and the renunciation of all former allegiances for citizenship.

1818

Regular sailing services between New York and Liverpool, England, begin; many emigrants from England, Ireland, and Germany embark from Liverpool.

1820

The United States begins recording the number and original country of residence of new immigrants.

1820–1860s

The first great wave of immigration to the United States begins. Most immigrants come from Ireland, Germany, or Scandinavia. Approximately 4.8 million people immigrate to the United States during this period.

1840

Immigration becomes even easier with regular steamship service between England and the United States.

1845

The American Party, an anti-immigrant, anti-Catholic party later known as the Know-Nothings, is founded.

1845–1847

The Irish potato famine leads to hundreds of thousands of Irish immigrating to the United States. Crop failures in Germany and the Netherlands also encourage emigration.

1849

The California gold rush begins following the discovery of gold at a German immigrant's camp. Significant Chinese migration to the United States begins.

1851–1860

The peak decade for Irish migration to the United States; official records show that 914,199 Irish arrived in the United States during this period.

1854

The Know-Nothing Party wins sweeping victories in national and state elections. The party's platform calls for limits on immigration and a twenty-one-year waiting period for citizenship.

1861–1865

Immigration falls off sharply during the American Civil War.

1862

The Homestead Act is passed by Congress to encourage the settlement of the West; it offers 160 acres of free land to anyone who settles and farms the land for five years.

1865–1869

The transcontinental railroad is built; many of the laborers are either Irish or Chinese immigrants.

1868

The Burlingame Treaty is ratified. The treaty permits unrestricted immigration by Chinese citizens to the United States, although they are not allowed to become U.S. citizens; the Fourteenth Amendment to the Constitution guarantees American citizenship to all people born on American soil.

1870

The Naturalization Act, which limits American citizenship to "white persons and persons of African descent," is passed. Asians are still not allowed to become citizens.

1875

The first federal law restricting immigration prohibits prostitutes, foreign convicts, and "involuntarily traveling orientals" from entering the United States.

1880–1920

The second wave of mass immigration begins with new groups from southern and eastern Europe.

1881–1890

The peak decade for German and Scandinavian immigration to the United States; the total number of German immigrants is 1,452,970; immigrants from Sweden, Norway, and Denmark number 656,494.

1882

The Chinese Exclusion Act—which limits the number of Chinese immigrant laborers to one hundred per year—is passed, effectively ending Chinese immigration to the United States. The act was renewed in 1892 and made permanent in 1902.

1886

The Statue of Liberty is dedicated in New York Harbor.

1891

Congress bans the immigration of "all idiots, insane persons, paupers or persons likely to become a public charge, persons suffering from a contagious or loathsome disease, persons who have been convicted of a felony or other infamous crime or misdemeanor involving moral turpitude, and polygamists."

1892

Ellis Island in New York Harbor is opened as the new immigration reception center; by 1932 Ellis Island had welcomed 12 million immigrants.

1894

The Immigration Restriction League (IRL) is formed in Boston, and Senator Henry Cabot Lodge soon becomes its leader. The IRL seeks to limit immigration to peoples of Nordic or northern European descent and works to pass a literacy test for entering immigrants.

1897

Congress passes a bill requiring all new immigrants to pass a literacy test; the bill is vetoed by President Grover Cleveland.

1905

The first year that more than 1 million immigrants arrive in the United States.

1907

The Gentleman's Agreement is reached between the United States and Japan. It stops Japanese immigration except for the wives of Japanese men already in the United States and prospective brides. Congress passes the Expatriation Act of 1907, which provides that an American woman, naturalized or native born, loses her citizenship upon marrying a foreigner.

1910

The Mexican Revolution sends hundreds of thousands of Mexicans across the border into the United States.

1913

Congress passes the Alien Land Law, which makes it illegal for noncitizens to purchase land; it is directed at the Issei, the first generation of Japanese Americans.

1914–1918

World War I interrupts mass immigration to the United States.

1917

Over President Woodrow Wilson's veto, Congress passes an immigration law that requires all immigrants over age sixteen to be literate; it also bans all emigration from Asia.

1921

The Emergency Immigration Act is passed; it establishes broad-based immigration restrictions based on national quotas. It places a limit of 350,000 immigrants per year, and only

3 percent of the foreign-born population of each nationality, according to the 1910 census, are to be allowed to immigrate annually.

1922

Congress passes the Cable Act, which nullifies the Expatriation Act of 1907 except as it applies to those American women who married "aliens ineligible to citizenship" (Asians).

1924

Congress passes the National Origins Act, which reduces the total number of potential immigrants to 350,000 annually and sets 1890 as the base year for determining the quota of those eligible. The quota itself is reduced from 3 percent to 2 percent of those migrants from any given country living in the United States as of 1890. Immigrants can also be inspected at their point of departure instead of their arrival point.

1943

The Chinese Exclusion Act is repealed.

1954

With immigrants going through inspection in their home country prior to departure, there is little need for the immigration station at Ellis Island; the inspection station closes its doors on November 19.

1965

The Immigration Act of 1965 removes the national origins quota system. It establishes a ceiling of 170,000 immigrants per year with a limit of 20,000 immigrants from any one country. It also creates a system of preferences, with the highest priority given to family reunification; the Ellis Island immigration station becomes a part of the Statue of Liberty National Monument. Restoration begins; the doors open to the public in 1976.

For Further Research

Edith Abbott, *Historical Aspects of the Immigration Problem: Select Documents.* Chicago: University of Chicago Press, 1926.

Jane Addams, *Twenty Years at Hull House.* New York: Macmillan, 1910.

Taylor Anbinder, *Nativism and Slavery: The Northern Know-Nothings and the Politics of the 1850s.* New York: Oxford University Press, 1992.

H. Arnold Barton, *Letters from the Promised Land.* Minneapolis: University of Minnesota Press, 1975.

Roy Howard Beck, *The Case Against Immigration: The Moral, Economic, Social, and Environmental Reasons for Reducing U.S. Immigration Back to Traditional Levels.* New York: W.W. Norton, 1996.

Marion Bennett, *American Immigration Policy: A History.* Washington, DC: Public Affairs, 1963.

John Bodnar, *The Transplanted: A History of Immigrants in Urban America.* Bloomington: Indiana University Press, 1985.

Peter Brimelow, *Alien Nation: Common Sense About America's Immigration Disaster.* New York: Random House, 1995.

David M. Brownstone, Irene M. Franck, and Douglass L. Brownstone, *Island of Hope, Island of Tears.* New York: Penguin, 1986.

Peter Morton Coan, *Ellis Island Interviews.* New York: Facts On File, 1997.

Roger Daniels, *Coming to America.* New York: HarperCollins, 1990.

Roger Daniels and Otis L. Graham, *Debating American Immigration, 1882–Present.* Lanham, MD: Rowman & Littlefield, 2001.

Philip Davis, ed., *Immigration and Americanization: Selected Readings.* Boston: Ginn, 1920.

Robert Divine, *American Immigration Policy, 1924–1952.* New Haven, CT: Yale University Press, 1957.

Richard M. Ebeling and Jacob G. Hornberger, eds., *The Case for Free Trade and Open Immigration.* Fairfax, VA: Future of Freedom Foundation, 1995.

Nathan Glazer and Daniel P. Moynihan, *Beyond the Melting Pot.* Cambridge, MA: MIT Press, 1963.

Madison Grant, *The Passing of the Great Race.* New York: Charles Scribner's, 1916.

Oscar Handlin, *This Was America.* Cambridge, MA: Harvard University Press, 1949.

John Higham, *Send These to Me: Immigrants in Urban America.* Baltimore, MD: Johns Hopkins University Press, 1984.

———, *Strangers in the Land.* New Brunswick, NJ: Rutgers University Press, 1955.

Irving Howe, *World of Our Fathers.* New York: Harcourt Brace Jovanovich, 1976.

Dale T. Knobel, *"America for the Americans": The Nativist Movement in the United States.* New York: Twayne, 1996.

Alan M. Kraut, *The Huddled Masses: The Immigrants in American Society, 1880–1921.* Arlington Heights, IL: Harlan Davidson, 1982.

Kerby Miller, *Emigrants and Exiles: Ireland and the Irish Exodus to North America.* New York: Oxford University Press, 1977.

Stuart C. Miller, *The Unwelcome Immigrant.* Berkeley: University of California Press, 1969.

John Millman, *The Other Americans: How Immigrants Renew Our Country, Our Economy, and Our Values.* New York: Viking Press, 1997.

Nicolaus Mills, ed., *Arguing Immigration: The Debate over the Changing Face of America*. New York: Simon and Schuster, 1994.

Joan Morrison and Charlotte Fox Zabusky, *American Mosaic: The Immigration Experience in the Words of Those Who Lived It*. New York: E.P. Dutton, 1990.

Thomas Muller and Thomas J. Espenshade, *The Fourth Wave: California's Newest Immigrants*. Washington, DC: Urban Institute Press, 1985.

Michael Novak, *Unmeltable Ethnics: Politics and Culture in American Life*. 2nd ed. New Brunswick, NJ: Transaction Publishers, 1996.

Juan F. Perea, ed., *Immigrants Out! The New Nativism and the Anti-Immigrant Impulse in the United States*. New York: New York University Press, 1997.

George E. Pozetta, ed., *American Immigration and Ethnicity*. 20 vols. New York: Garland, 1991.

Jacob Riis, *How the Other Half Lives*. Cambridge, MA: Harvard University Press, 1910.

Josiah Strong, *Our Country*. Ed. Jurgen Herbst. Cambridge, MA: Belknap Press of Harvard University Press, 1963.

William Tefft and Thomas Dunne, *Ellis Island*. New York: W.W. Norton, 1971.

Thomas C. Wheeler, ed., *The Immigrant Experience: The Anguish of Becoming American*. New York: Penguin, 1971.

Chilton Williamson, *The Immigration Mystique: America's False Conscience*. New York: BasicBooks, 1996.

✸ Index

(1851–1864), 184
They Who Knock at Our Gates
(Antin), 71
Tocqueville, Alexis de, 114
Turner, Frederick Jackson, 120
Tweed, William M. "Boss,"
113

United States
belongs to Americans, 44–47
Chinese immigration
benefits to, 135–40
con, 127–34
complex idea of, 49–51
has a national ethnicity,
193–202
con, 203–11
immigrants endanger,
27–35, 57–63, 109–14,
153–56
con, 36–43, 64–74
motto of, 220
1910 population
demographics in, 97
was built by immigrants,
209–10

Virginia Gazette (newspaper),
10
voting rights
are used for political
purposes, 29
need safeguards, 89
see also citizenship

wages
in China vs. California, 131
immigrants depress, 61, 77,
132, 152
con, 136–37
Walker, Francis A., 57
War Brides Act (1944), 181
War of 1812, 11
Washington, George, 46
Weisberger, Bernard A., 203
Weismann, August, 99
Whitney, Craig, 221
Williamson, Jeffrey G., 120
Wilson, Pete, 204
Wilson, Woodrow, 20, 21, 126
Wright, Carroll D., 77

Zangwill, Israel, 108, 213